Highlights for Children
Growing Up Reading

I caen ReD

Highlights for Children

Growing Up Reading

Sharing with Your Children the Joys of Reading

Linda Leonard Lamme, Ph.D.
Foreword by Walter B. Barbe, Ph.D., Editor-in-Chief, *Highlights for Children*

ACROPOLIS BOOKS LTD.
WASHINGTON, D.C.

© Copyright 1985, Highlights ® for Children, Inc. All rights reserved. Except for the inclusion of brief quotations in a review, no part of this book may be reproduced or utilized in any form or by any means, electronic or mechanical, including photocopying, recording, or by any information storage and retrieval system, without permission in writing from the publisher.

ACROPOLIS BOOKS, Ltd.
Colortone Building, 2400 17th Street, N.W.
Washington, D.C. 20009

Printed in the United States of America by
COLORTONE PRESS
Creative Graphics, Inc.
Washington, D.C. 20009

Attention: Schools and Corporations
ACROPOLIS books are available at quantity discounts with bulk purchase for educational, business, or sales promotional use. For further information, please write to: SPECIAL SALES DEPARTMENT, ACROPOLIS BOOKS, LTD., 2400 17th ST., N.W., WASHINGTON, D.C. 20009.

Are there Acropolis Books you want but cannot find in your local stores?
You can get any Acropolis book title in print. Simply send title and retail price, plus 50 cents for postage and handling costs for each book desired. District of Columbia residents add applicable sales tax. Enclose check or money order only, no cash please, to: ACROPOLIS BOOKS, LTD., 2400 17th ST., N.W., WASHINGTON, D.C. 20009.

Photo Credits
Gene Gisson: pp. 13-15, 31, 45, 48, 50, 52, 56, 58, 62, 68, 70, 71, 75, 77, 78, 84-85, 99, 101, 102, 103, 105, 111, 116, 160; Ary J. Lamme III: pp. 16, 22, 42, 108, 148, 149, 150, 151, 153, 158; Michelle Plumley: p. 25; J. Terry Gaffney: pp. 28, 47; Herb Press: pp. 30, 32, 34, 37, 40, 43, 46, 51, 55, 59, 79, 92, 113-115, 117, 126, 128, 129, 132, 133, 135, 136, 137, 142, 143, 146, 208; Jim Condon: p. 53; John R. Crane: pp. 63, 166, 168, 170, 173, 176, 180, 183, 186, 188, 190; Ron Dunnivan: p. 96; WNED-TV, Buffalo, New York: p. 119.

A grateful acknowledgement for the following permissions: P. 39 "The Reading Mother" by Strickland Gillilan reproduced with permission of John F. Carroll, Carroll Book Service, Inc., North Tarrytown, New York; p. 41 "Hi and Lois" reprinted with special permission of King Features Syndicate, Inc.; pp. 44, 67, 90, "The Family Circus" reprinted courtesy of Cowles Syndicate, Inc. All rights reserved; pp. 63-65 Book list from the book, *For Reading Out Loud! A Guide to Sharing Books with Children*, by Margaret Mary Kimmel and Elizabeth Segel. Copyright © 1983 by Margaret Mary Kimmel and Elizabeth Segel. Reprinted by permission of Delacorte Press.

Library of Congress Cataloging in Publication Data

Lamme, Linda Leonard.
  Growing Up Reading.

  Written in cooperation with the children's magazine,
Highlights for Children.
  Includes index.
  1. Children—Books and reading.
  I. Highlights for Children, Inc. II. Title.
  Z1037.A1L225   1985   649'.58   85-7333
  ISBN 0-87491-777-8

Dedication
**For my husband, Ary,
my daughter, Laurel Agnes,
and my son, Ary**

Acknowledgements

I appreciate the support I received from many people while I was writing this book. My husband and daughter provided much of the incentive for the project. The teachers, parents, and students I have worked with have shared with me many ideas that appear throughout the book. The children's librarians, especially Linda Boyles, Rosie Russo, and Vicki Ward, at Santa Fe Regional Library in Gainesville, Florida, and the librarians at Cazenovia Public Library have been helpful way beyond the call of duty. A special thank-you to Buffy Bondy and Nora Hoover at the University of Florida, and to Maureen Rickard and the editors and staff at *Highlights* and Acropolis.

Contents

Foreword	9
Introduction	11
1 How Reading Begins	13

Oral Language Development . . . The Sounds of Language . . . The Structure of Language . . . The Meaning of Language . . . Kidwatching . . . Oral Language Activities . . . Learning the Alphabet . . . ABC Books . . . Beginning-to-Read Books

2 Reading Aloud with Children	39

Why Read Aloud? . . . General Guidelines . . . Age-Specific Guidelines . . . Books for Reading Aloud . . . References on Reading Aloud

3 Reading Comprehension	67

Levels of Comprehension . . . Comprehension Strategies . . . Parental Concerns

| 4 | Word Recognition | 81 |

Context ... Sight Words ... Key Words ... Structural Analysis ... Configuration ... Phonics

| 5 | Reading Is Everywhere | 95 |

Cooking ... Shopping ... Traveling ... Music ... Following Directions ... Writing and Reading ... Television

| 6 | Reading Strengths and Weaknesses | 125 |

Observing Children ... Children Who Experience Difficulty Reading ... Children Who Read Early ... Every Child Is Gifted

| 7 | Maintaining Reading Habits | 145 |

Developing Routine Reading Times ... Developing the Library Habit ... Children's Magazines ... Purchasing Books ... Broadening Reading Interests ... Extending Books with Other Activities

| 8 | Books Too Good to Miss | 165 |

Book Review Sources ... Book Awards ... Book Recommendations

Conclusion	193
Appendix	195
Index	203

Foreword

The home is the first and most important learning environment of all. It is parents who have the major responsibility for instilling in their children a love of reading that will last all their lives. In my thirty years as a teacher, professor, and editor of *Highlights for Children,* I have never lost this conviction.

Highlights for Children is proud to have worked with Professor Linda Lamme on *Growing Up Reading.* It is a book that provides for parents the means of sharing the joy of reading with their children.

A professor of early childhood education, Dr. Linda Lamme shares our belief that children begin to develop reading skills in infancy; and they will learn naturally when surrounded by people who love to read, who read to them, and who respond to their questions with care and enthusiasm.

Dr. Lamme has made *Growing Up Reading* a book of insights and activities, not a formal reading program. Families will find this book filled with "fun with a purpose" ideas children can enjoy from infancy through elementary school.

Growing Up Reading will be a valuable addition to your family. It is the companion volume to *Growing Up Writing,* also by

Dr. Lamme. Both books can make a real difference in your home. As one eight-year-old said recently, "Some families are good at music, and some are good at dancing. Ours is good at reading."

Walter B. Barbe, Ph.D.
Editor-in-Chief, *Highlights for Children*

Introduction

When my daughter was born, I was curious—even a bit concerned. I wondered when and how Laurel would learn to read. Both my husband and I are avid readers and, if there was anything we wanted to ensure, it was that our daughter would develop a love of reading as well. Having a baby in the family was my opportunity to practice what I had been teaching in college classes for a number of years. When Laurel grew naturally into reading with little conscious effort on our part, I was filled with awe. I kept careful records of how she progressed and what we had done to promote her love of reading. The whole process was so effortless and so enjoyable that I feel compelled to share those experiences with parents.

People often ask when I began to read to Laurel. I reply, "Well, I guess the first time was the day she was born when I sang hymns out loud." Of course, I was really singing for myself as well. Hymns tend to ease my discomfort. Both my husband and I did read, talk, and sing to Laurel right from the beginning. We also wrote for her in manuscript writing and gave her many opportunities to scribble, draw, and write. As I look back on them, these activities appear to be the keys to her growing up reading.

In addition to my own experiences with Laurel, I have read the professional literature on reading to support the teaching I do at the University of Florida and the workshops I give for parents and teachers. This book contains the answers to questions I am most frequently asked at those workshops. It is a combination, then, of my personal experience as a parent and my professional experience as a teacher.

Growing Up Reading shares many ideas for encouraging a love of reading from birth through the elementary school years.

I have two fundamental biases about learning to read. They are that
—the home is the first and most important learning environment that a child will ever have, and
—reading ability develops naturally from a love of reading.

Parents don't need to worry about "teaching" their children to read. Children will learn to read naturally if they are surrounded by adults who enjoy reading, who read to their children, and who are responsive to their children's curiosity about print.

There are many references to children's books in *Growing Up Reading*. You can find these books at libraries and bookstores. If a book is not available in hardback, it is probably in paperback. Books do go out of print rather rapidly, however, so some of these books may be available only at libraries. I have tried to select books that are of high quality and popular enough to last. You can write to publishers to inquire about the current status of books that they publish. A list of publishers appears in the Appendix.

One of the problems with writing a book is that it is difficult to gauge the reaction of readers. If you would like to share your reactions or ask questions please write to me:

Linda L. Lamme, Ph.D.
Department of Elementary and Early Childhood Education
2215 Norman Hall
University of Florida
Gainesville, Florida 32611

I love to get mail (and I do promise a response).

Chapter 1

How Reading Begins

Two-year-old in car seat, as car drives past McDonald's, "Daddy, hamburger?"

Toddler, after Mother has just read a story, "More book, *please*."

One day I observed a mother reading nursery rhymes to her six-week-old infant. When the mother came to a rhyme that she had sung to the child since birth, the baby wiggled and

It's never too early to introduce books to your child.

Growing Up Reading 13

grinned. He obviously recognized the familiar rhyme, at only six weeks of age!

Children are learning to read from the day they are born. They have a natural desire to learn and are innately curious about language, both oral and written. When adults respond to this natural inclination on the part of children, learning to read becomes as natural a process as learning to talk.

One night a father was parked in a shopping center parking lot with his two-year-old. To pass the time, he was pointing out the neon store signs to the child. All of a sudden the child pointed and exclaimed, "Stop!" The father looked across the parking lot and saw a store sign that read KWIK STOP. That child had really read the sign! She had found the familiar word she had seen so frequently on hexagonal stop signs in a totally different setting!

Bit by bit, children become skilled at reading the print in their environment.

So often we think that children cannot read until they are reading whole books. Children far younger than school age are reading. Bit by bit, they are becoming more skilled at interpreting print. Our job as parents is to recognize what our children can do and convince them that they can read.

Even tiny children believe that they can read when they recognize the titles of books, words on street signs, and the names of their friends. This positive approach to learning to

When they recognize the titles of books, even very young children feel like readers.

read builds children's self-concepts and takes away the pressures associated with learning how to read. If you can read a little, it is easy to learn how to read a little more; but if you cannot read at all, reading is a big mystery. This can be frightening to little children.

Parents sometimes hear the term "reading readiness" used to indicate that period of time just prior to real reading. Reading is actually a gradual process that begins at birth. Children learn at vastly different rates. You as a parent have a tremendous impact upon the ease with which your child learns to read. Our discussion in this chapter will involve all the years from birth to beginning reading, whenever beginning to read may happen for any one child.

Oral Language Development

Oral language is the basis upon which reading (and writing to some extent) is built. Children who are most fluent in oral language have the easiest time learning how to read. They also enjoy social advantages, for they can explain their feelings and thoughts more easily.

Although children learn language as a whole, a useful way for adults to think about oral language development is to classify development into three areas: the sounds of language, the structure of language, and the meaning of language. There are ways in which parents can enhance children's development in each of these areas.

The Sounds of Language

When children are born, they have the capacity to produce any sound in any language in the world. Within the first year, however, they lose the capacity to produce easily any sound that is not in the language of those speaking to them. For example,

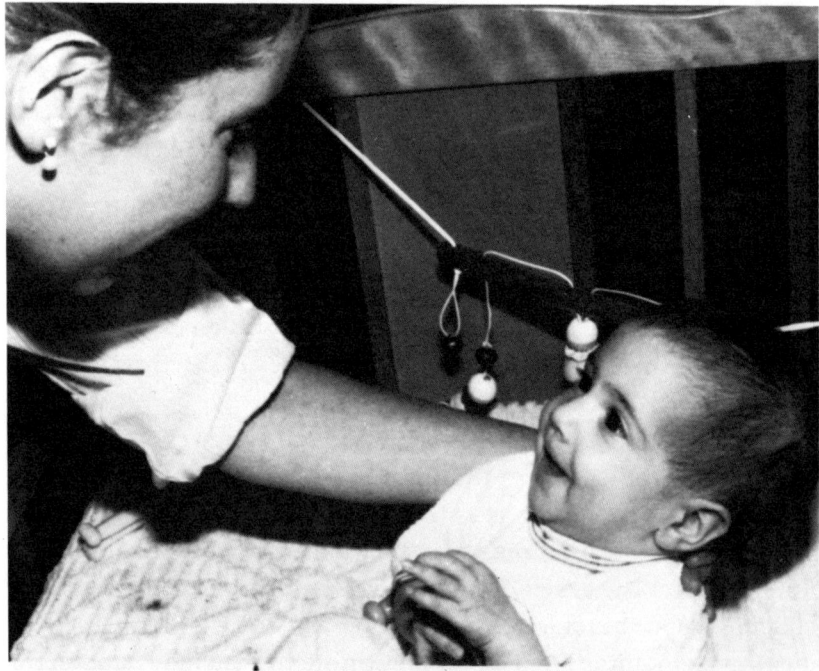

As babies listen and enjoy talk, they learn that language is a social tool.

American children are unable to make German gutteral throat sounds, and Japanese children have difficulty with *r* sounds. By school age, American children are able to produce practically all the sounds in the English language and to blend them together into almost any word that an adult can pronounce.

The first sounds that a child makes are called babbles. As early as the first day of life, babies make sounds as they cry and coo. Adults can encourage this sound-making by a technique the late Ira Gordon called "Ping-Pong." Gordon, a prominent early childhood educator, said that adults should respond when their babies make a sound by repeating that sound back to the baby. What often happens, then, is that the baby returns the sound, and a ping-pong effect has taken place. Thus, the baby learns that language is a social tool.

From babbling, babies learn to make one-syllable sounds which are often repeated: da-da-da. These sounds can represent words (*daddy*). Children learn to make initial consonant sounds before they learn blends. Gradually they put more and more sounds together into words.

Another idea promoted by Gordon is to place the baby in a "language envelope" during the first years. Surround the baby with language. As you are diapering, bathing, or carrying your baby about, you can be talking and singing to him or her. Some parents feel silly talking to a baby who does not respond, yet your baby most certainly is listening to you and enjoying your talk.

Every adult needs a good comprehensive Mother Goose collection as well as a collection of fingerplays and songs that will enhance the child's awareness of language sounds. Once there is a large source of chants and songs, it becomes easy to match the chant to the activity of the child. Repeating rhymes over and over again gives babies and young children a chance to memorize the chants and sing along with them.

Following are some songs and chants to accompany daily routines. You may have other favorites. These little ditties and songs liven up your days and make even the most repetitious chores seem more interesting and fun. You can personalize them by substituting your child's name or another activity for the words in the rhyme.

Along with chanting and singing old favorite songs, you can make up some of our own. These evolve from just making word substitutions to making up lyrics to familiar tunes. From "This is the way we wash our clothes" in "Mulberry Bush," can come: "This is the way we ride our bike," or "This is the way we brush our teeth." From "Are you sleeping?" can come: "Are you eating?" "Are you coming?" or "Are you happy?"

Songs and Chants to Accompany Daily Routines

Waking Up in the Morning
Wake up Jacob
  Day's a breakin'
Peas in the pot
  and hoecakes abakin'

Feeding
Pease porridge hot,
Pease porridge cold,
Pease porridge in the pot,
Nine days old.
Some like it hot,
Some like it cold,
Some like it in the pot,
Nine days old.

Bathing
This is the way we wash our face,
  wash our face,
  wash our face,
This is the way we wash our face
  so early Monday morning.
(Repeat with each body part: scrub our ears, etc.)

Dressing
Oh, here's a leg for a stocking,
And here's a foot for a shoe,
And he has a kiss for his daddy,
And two for his mammy, I trow.

When Something Is Lost
Oh where, oh where has my little dog gone? (substitute)
Oh where, oh where can he be?
With his ears cut short and his tail cut long,
Oh where, oh where can he be?

Riding in the Car
The wheels of the car go round and round
  round and round
  round and round
The wheels of the car go round and round
  all around the town.
(Repeat with: washers go swish, swish, swish;
        horn goes beep, beep, beep, etc.)

Going Shopping
To market, to market
To buy a fat pig (substitute here)
Home again, home again
Jiggety jig.

    To market, to market
    To buy a fat hog
    Home again, home again
    Jiggety jog.

        To market, to market
        To buy a plum bun;
        Home again, home again,
        Market is done.

Going to Bed
Diddle, diddle, dumpling, my son John
Went to bed with his breeches on;
One shoe off and the other shoe on,
Diddle, diddle, dumpling, my son John.

Wee Willie Winkie runs through the town,
Upstairs and downstairs in his nightgown,
Rapping at the window, crying through the lock,
"Are the children in their beds?
For now it's eight o'clock."

    There are many rhyming games that can be played while doing routine chores or riding in the car with a preschooler. Reading lots of poetry provides models which children can emulate. After reading *'I Can't,' Said the Ant*, make up endless rhymes of your own:

"Let's hug," said the rug.

"Where's your hat?" asked the cat.

"Don't fall!" cried the doll.

"Oh no!" cried the crow.

Children begin recognizing similar beginnings to words when they know a lot of names, some of which begin the same way. Then, games can be made of alliteration:

"Larry likes lemons."

"Susan sings songs."

"Tanya takes the train."

The essence of all these activities is that they make children conscious of language sounds. Children learn that they have powerful control over their own language and that oral language play can be enjoyable. It is rare that children who have been sung to since infancy are not found humming to themselves while they are playing. Not long ago I visited a kindergarten classroom where the children were making collages for an art activity and over half of the children were quietly humming to themselves as they worked. There is a natural inclination on the part of young children to sing and talk as they play. Children give themselves natural drills with oral language, rhyming things just for fun. Play is the natural stimulation of oral language, especially if children grow up in an oral language environment that immerses them in talking and singing when they are with adults.

The Structure of Language

The structure of language is defined as the way the words fit together into sentences to contain meaning. We used to think that children learned to talk by copying their parents, but it is evident, since children can create many sentences that they have never heard before, that learning sentence structure is a far more complex task than mere imitation. Children are actively processing language and intuitively discovering the underlying grammatical structures that give meaning to language. One would never hear a child, even a very young child utter, "Dog the ran road the down." Somehow even at very young ages, children have learned that the subject precedes the verb. Children don't learn the rules, but they internalize the rules and use them in their speech.

Children's speech develops from saying one word, called a holophrase, which stands for many words or a whole idea, to speaking long sentences. For example, when a baby says "wauwau" (water), the interpretation might be, "Mother, I am very thirsty and would appreciate a glass of water immediately." The mother does not question the child's intent and quickly produces the water for the baby. One word communicates the whole concept.

Next, the child puts two words together in what is termed "telegraphic speech." The language is similar to what one would send in a telegram, omitting all of the unimportant words in the expression so that the meaning is clear from the words that remain. "Go store," means, "I want to go to the store with you." Again, telegraphic speech communicates very clearly when we listen to it carefully.

Gradually, the young child begins to add adjectives, adverbs, and direct objects to simple sentences. Instead of being just two words long, sentences become three and four words long. A popular book by Bill Martin, Jr., *Brown Bear, Brown Bear, What Do You See?* provides good examples of simple sentences.

"Brown bear, brown bear, what do you see?
I see a yellow bird, looking at me.
Yellow bird, yellow bird, what do you see? . . . "

This little book helps children acquire the use of adjectives (in this case, color words), questions, and answers.

A big jump in language development comes when children begin to add dependent clauses to their language. A dependent clause (for those who have long since forgotten high school English grammar classes) is a subject and a predicate that is dependent upon the rest of the sentence for meaning. For example, one might say, "It is a gorgeous day." Adding a dependent clause gives you the sentence "When the sun shines like this, it is a gorgeous day." When children begin to use words like *because, on account of, before, after, when,* and *if,* their sentences are not only longer, but more complex.

One object of your language interactions with your baby or

young child, then, is to expand the number of words in sentences. This may be done in a variety of ways.

One method of elaboration for babies is called scaffolding, where adults supply words for the baby who cannot yet say them. If the baby coos and is looking at a ball, the parent might say, "Yes, see that red ball," or "You'd like the red ball," and then give the ball to the child. In this example, the parent not only supplies the unknown (or at least unintelligible) word but also puts the word in context for the child.

Similarly, adults expand the condensed language of children. If the child says, "Want snack," the parent who is expanding the child's language will respond, "Oh, you're hungry and you'd like a snack." Another positive result of expanding a child's language is what Thomas Gordon in *Parent Effectiveness Training* (New American Library, 1970) calls "active listening." When you repeat, essentially, what the child has said in different terminology, you are letting the child know that you are really listening to him or her. You are double-checking

During library story hours, children often participate in action rhymes and fingerplays.

whether you really did understand the child, which opens up communication between the two of you. There is a chance to correct false impressions, to get the "message behind the message," and to let the child realize that you care what he or she says.

Books with longer sentence patterns provide good models. Book talk is not the same as oral language. Children who have listened to a lot of literature reveal those more complex structures in their speech. A child peering out the second story window in an airport terminal was heard to say, "I'm as very high as I can be." Clearly he had heard this phrasing from a storybook.

Rhymes, chants, fingerplays, and other language games stimulate expanded language as well. There are several excellent sources of songs and fingerplays. It is helpful if song collections include the music and chords for each song. You might use several comprehensive collections to play and sing at the piano and several smaller collections to take for singing in the car. A church hymnal is another favorite songbook. Here are three excellent song and fingerplay collections:

Eye Winker, Tom Tinker, Chin Chopper, by Tom Glazer. (New York: Doubleday, 1973). A collection of fifty musical fingerplays.

Wee Sing, by Pamela C. Beall and Susan H. Nipp. (Los Angeles: Price/Stern/Sloan, 1981, 1982, 1983). A series of small paperback songbooks with both music and lyrics. Separate books come for silly songs, camp songs, and fingerplays.

Heritage Songster, by Leon and Lynn Dallin. (Dubuque, Iowa: W. C. Brown, 1980). Contains 332 folk songs and familiar songs with music and chords—a comprehensive collection.

Another influence upon children's sentence development is the type of questions adults ask children. Most of the time children are asked questions that have only one-word answers. "Did you like school today?" "What did you play at Tom's house?" The adult who wants to expand children's responses, however, will increase the number of questions that call for explanation or discussion. Questions that begin with words such as "Why?" "How?" or "Tell me about . . . " are likely to get longer responses than the who-what-where-when types of questions that require only a one-word reply.

Growing Up Reading

As children learn to talk, they say, "We swam in the ocean," because that is what they have heard adults say. Later, as children begin to construct more of the rules internally, they say, "We swimmed in the ocean." They have used the rule for adding *ed* to a word to change it to past tense. But this happens to be an overgeneralization of the rule. The word *swim* is an exception. As children get more advanced in language usage, they will hear the word *swam* used more often and will refine their speech to the correct use of the past tense.

Should adults correct children in cases where they overgeneralize? Probably not. Children who are constantly corrected will talk less. Further, the correction won't lead to a change in the child's talk. Criticism makes children less secure, less self-confident, and less willing to take risks. Learning a language requires that children take many risks and try out their language even if they are not sure it is correct. Only by comparing their talk with the talk of elders do they notice the disparities and refine their phrases—or sentences. Not until they are considerably older (in school) can their language be refined or corrected without having an impact upon its acquisition.

The Meaning of Language

Parents often use baby talk with their children, simplifying terminology they consider too technical for a child to understand. It would be wiser to use the accurate term in every case. The more words children know, the more words they take with them to the reading experience. If they already know the meanings of most of the words in print, learning to read will come easily.

When children learn words, they often overgeneralize the categories to which the words apply. John Holt gives an excellent example of this in his book *How Children Learn* (Pittman, 1966). His daughter, at one point when they were driving through the country, called a horse a cow. Instead of correcting her and telling her, "No, that was a horse," he realized that the child had overgeneralized, thinking that all four-legged animals in a pasture were cows. Instead, he repeatedly talked about the horses they were passing in other pastures and, before long, the child was differentiating between the two four-legged creatures on her own. Had Holt corrected his daughter, what could have happened? The child might have said to herself, "I am not sure what that four-legged animal is, so I better not risk being wrong." Children who are corrected a lot become less verbal, developing less extensive oral vocabularies than children who are not corrected.

As children help with routine activities, they learn specialized vocabulary.

Direct experiences, such as trips in the car and visits to various places, are wonderful enhancers of vocabulary. Museums, concerts, and festivals expand children's vocabularies through exposure to new experiences and activities. Having children help with routine activities, such as cooking, sewing, making repairs, cleaning, and folding laundry, helps them learn specialized vocabulary.

After one parent had read the phrase "Be sensible" in a book, his son used that term many times in different contexts, most of which were appropriate. We are not often aware of the impact of literature on vocabulary because so often children use terms found in books and we don't notice them. It is only when children make mistakes that their use of these terms becomes obvious.

In today's television age, many children come to school with large vocabularies gleaned from TV. But children fool us. They can pronounce many words that they don't really understand. There's no substitute for a broad range of experiences supplemented by reading and conversation with adults to help children's vocabularies grow in depth.

Playing word games is a good way to pass the time with your child. Preschoolers enjoy games like "Bigger Than," where each person thinks of something bigger than the last person, or "Color Words," where players take turns thinking of something green (or another color). Older children like "Password," "I'm Taking a Trip to China" (where each person adds something to the list of luggage) and "Gossip" or "Telephone" games. These games do two things: they develop language and thinking skills, and they develop positive attitudes toward learning through play.

There are several strategies that inhibit the growth of language in young children. Correction has already been mentioned as having a negative effect. Another way *not* to build vocabulary is to drill children with word cards. Just as with learning words on TV, learning with word cards is superficial. Children may learn to pronounce new words, but they won't actually incorporate the words into their speech. Other negative practices include talking over children's heads or spelling words so the children will not understand the adult conversation. Aside from being poor manners, such practices remove the incentive for learning language. If adults wish to conduct exclusive conversations, they should do so in private. A final negative behavior on the part of parents is to laugh at children's language or to make remarks such as, "Isn't that cute?" Belittling comments can encourage baby talk or stunt creativity, a necessary element in language development.

Kidwatching

Yetta Goodman, a professor of education at Arizona State University, urges parents and teachers of young children to become what she terms "kidwatchers."

Kidwatching is enjoyable and enlightening. More important, kidwatching makes us sensitive to children's talk. You become more aware of what your child knows and doesn't know, of what your child can say and can't say, and therefore are more able to know how to assist with language development.

If you hear a child say "hauter" for "water" and "het" for "wet," you know that the child cannot make the *w* sound yet. You might arrange for some chants and fingerplays which use the *w* sound: "Water, water, everywhere and not a drop to drink," for example, or the song "Little Sally Waters." With practice at using that sound in a nonthreatening situation, the child will acquire the new sound in time.

If you heard your child say, "I learned him how to skip," you might respond, "You taught him how to skip—how wonderful!" letting the child know you shared in his delight while at the same time modeling the correct use of the word *taught*. If you heard your child say, "That sure is a little horse," the adult might explain to the child that a small horse is called a pony and share a rhyme about a pony, like "Pony Boy." In short, kidwatching provides information so that you can become a more effective teacher of your child.

Oral Language Activities

There are numerous oral language activities that generally stimulate language development. Singing and chanting have already been discussed. Generally, talking with children and explaining things to them help develop verbal children. Listening to children talk, and particularly to the messages they are communicating, is one of the best ways to encourage language development. If children have an attentive audience, they will almost always talk. Providing many direct experiences to talk about and share together—experiences like gardening, painting, cooking, and playing games—is the core of good language development. Other, more special opportunities which specifically provide for talk can be provided.

Storytelling
In the past, storytelling played a prominent part in the upbringing of children. Stories were told to transmit the

cultural heritage, to provide moral lessons, to entertain families after supper, and to develop the self-confidence of the storyteller. Today, books, television, and other recreational activities have almost obliterated the art of storytelling from our culture, except for performances at folk festivals. Yet storytelling remains an important contributor to children's oral language development and reading readiness.

Why is storytelling important? It enhances children's vocabulary and language development. It helps children learn the sequence of a story—a sort of story awareness—which helps them anticipate the way a story might go. The ability to predict what might happen in a story is an important reading activity.

There are two types of stories your child can learn to tell. One is the retelling of a familiar fairy tale or folktale. By hearing the story read over and over again, your child will learn to retell the story. If you provide props, such as flannel-board characters, puppets, or dress-up props, it will be easier to tell the story.

A flannel board can be made by attaching flannel or felt to a rather large piece of heavy cardboard. If the cardboard is light, it will be portable. Characters for stories can be made out of felt or

Flannel-board characters help children retell favorite fairy tales or folktales.

cardboard with sandpaper attached to the back for adhesion. Pellon interfacing, used to line fabrics, adheres well to flannel and is transparent enough to trace characters from the pictures in a book. You can make puppets from socks, paper bags, and popsicle sticks. Props need not be complex. In fact, the simpler they are, the more imagination is required for their use.

You can help your child learn to tell a story by first telling the story along with a book—reading the pictures as clues to what happens next. You can tape-record the story as a background for your child to move the flannel board or puppet characters. Soon your child will be able to retell the story independently, first with and later without props.

Some good stories for acting out include:
The Three Bears
The Three Billy Goats Gruff
The Gunniwolf
Little Red Riding Hood
The Princess and the Pea
Rapunzel
Drakestail
Too Much Noise
Where the Wild Things Are
The Little Red Hen

A second type of storytelling is the telling of an original tale. You will enjoy telling your children stories about things that happened when you were young or when the children were younger. In some cases, these stories become the child's first history lessons. You might like to make up stories about children's toys, similar to the Winnie-the-Pooh or Paddington Bear stories. Sometimes these stories can have continuous episodes from day to day. You might want to tape-record or write down some of the stories you invent. Good storytelling requires a lot of adult modeling to be really effective.

Tape Recorder
Most children love to tape-record themselves and to hear their own language played back to them. The tape recorder is an excellent tool for language growth. You and your child might make tapes periodically to be sent to grandparents, other

relatives, or friends. On tape your child might sing songs, tell stories, read a book, or tell family news. Years later, children can play back the tapes and listen to what they sounded like when they were younger.

Play
Play greatly assists children's language development. Providing regular opportunities for your child to interact with other children gives opportunities for pretend play and for solving social problems orally. There are several types of play experiences which are especially good for enhancing language.

Playing with blocks and construction toys encourages children to share and make decisions together.

Blocks and other building toys encourage children to share materials, influence each other, and make decisions together about what they are going to construct. In addition, constructions are typically used for imaginative play when they have been completed—another opportunity for practice with vocabulary and oral language. For example, after building a garage, two children returned several times to "fix" their cars and to pump gas. It has been shown that many problem-solving situations arise during block play and that some children are far more adept than others at joining in the play and at swaying others to their points of view. The number and size of the materials available for construction also influence the quality of the interactions. It is best if children have play opportunities with several different sizes and types of construction materials.

Sand and water play are very appealing to young children. When you go to the beach, have your child take a friend and some digging toys and play vehicles. The children will entertain themselves for hours. You can make a sandbox outdoors by putting sand in a children's wading pool. On a rainy day a bathtub or sink full of water with funnels, toys, and floating and nonfloating items provides stimulation for lots of play and talk. Sand and water environments allow children to manipulate their play space, setting the stage for many kinds of pretend play. Children especially enjoy playing with dolls and toy people in sand and water environments.

Pretend play greatly enhances language. Given an appropriate play space (a large box, a blanket over a card table, or some other tentlike structure), most children play house with dolls, toys, or household items. This type of play allows children

Give them an appropriate space, and most children will play house— adopting the language of adults they know.

to role play, adopting the language that different adults typically use. When you listen to this type of play, you often hear remarkably accurate imitations of yourself!

A similar type of dramatic play occurs when children use props to enact fairy tales or other stories that require costumes. Jonathan and Scott played fire fighter for over a year, donning their fire hats, jackets, and rubber boots. They responded to one pretend emergency after another and acquired a rather sophisticated level of specialized fire squad vocabulary. By supplying simple props for this type of pretend play, adults provide the opportunity for imaginative role-playing. Dress-up props might include scarves, glasses (rims), jewelry, hats, old clothing, and shoes.

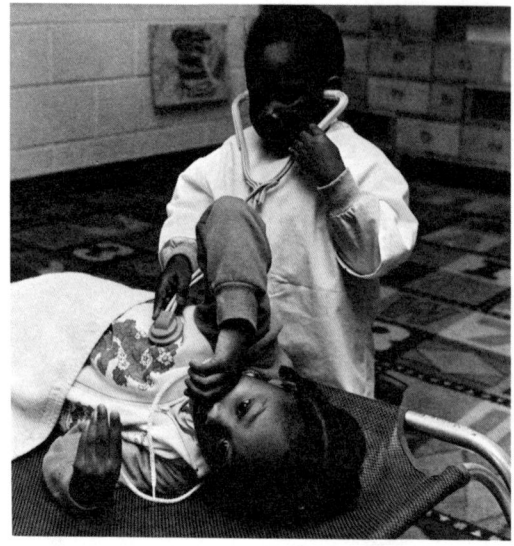

With their dress-up props and special vocabulary, youngsters enjoy hours of imaginative role-playing.

You should intervene as little as possible in children's play so that they have the opportunity to work out their own disagreements. When an adult does intervene, it should be to clarify issues so that children can make decisions which will solve the problem rather than to tell them what to do. Decision making is in itself an excellent way to clarify emotions through the use of language. Also, by lightly supervising play experiences, adults can listen to the oral language and learn a lot about levels of social and language development.

Learning the Alphabet

Most children learn how to recite the alphabet long before they learn how to read, causing adults to believe that learning the alphabet is a necessary prerequisite to learning how to read. This is not the case. Learning the alphabet is helpful for writing development, for if children know the alphabet and can recognize letters, they are better able to invent spellings or to have adults spell words orally for them. There are examples, however, of children who could not recognize alphabet letters but who could read a rather large number of words. One child began kindergarten a few weeks late in the term. She did not know her alphabet and could recognize and name only a few letters. The first day she was in kindergarten the children were writing love notes to each other, for they had learned how to write, "I love you." Natasha watched these children write and quickly learned how to read, "I love you." The following day one of the other children asked a small group, "How do you write *love?*" to which Natasha replied, "I'll show! I'll show you!" On a scrap of paper Natasha wrote *LOVE* and said, "Here, you can copy mine." At this point Natasha could not recognize any of the individual letters within the word, but she could read and write the word itself.

Natasha's case is an unusual one, but it does demonstrate that alphabet letter recognition is not a prerequisite for reading. Children can recognize whole words without knowing the names or sounds of the alphabet letters within them.

Most young children begin asking questions about the alphabet when they are far younger than Natasha. One child, for example, found the alphabet written on the endpapers of an alphabet book. She pointed to the alphabet letters, asking what they were until she had memorized most of them. The first letter she learned was *O*. The following day, while she was circling the block in her stroller, she spied an *O* in the stop sign. The next day, while playing with the telephone, she discovered another *O* on the dial, and so forth. She was not directly taught the alphabet and not asked to memorize it, but through her own curiosity she encountered the alphabet in many places and gradually came to recognize most of its letters.

Children enjoy singing the alphabet song. A good way to

have children learn the alphabet is to point to each letter while they are singing that song, so that they learn to match each letter with the letters they can already say. Magnetic alphabet letters that can be used to create short messages on the refrigerator door are another good way to play with the alphabet.

Magnetic letters encourage children to play with the alphabet.

While learning the alphabet, children also learn that some letters have certain sounds associated with them. It is helpful if children recognize these sounds within existing words rather than learn them in isolation. They play games such as "T is for Timmy, Terry, and turtle."

ABC Books

Children enjoy looking at ABC books. An especially good one is the *A to Z Picture Book* by Gyo Fujikawa (a book that is also superb for helping infants and toddlers expand their vocabularies). In this book, pictures of things starting with the same letter are labeled and grouped on the same pages.

If you want to expose your child to alphabet letter sounds, select ABC books that use consistent and commonly used initial sounds—*puppy* for the letter *p* instead of *plate,* which has a blend for the initial sound. Alphabet books use words to label the pictures so that children can identify the letters in the printed word as well as the picture/word relationship. Your child will notice some of the obvious inconsistencies in the English language (especially that *g* and *c* have two sounds and that the *k*, *s*, and *j* sounds can be represented by more than one letter).

Children enjoy making their own ABC books, drawing pictures or cutting up magazines to illustrate them. You can label the pictures.

The following is a list of high-quality ABC books.

Boynton, Sandra. *A Is for Angry*. New York: Workman, 1983.

Fujikawa, Gyo. *A to Z Picture Book*. New York: Grosset & Dunlap, 1974.

Hague, Kathleen. *Alphabears*. New York: Holt, Rinehart & Winston, 1983.

Lear, Edward. *An Edward Lear Alphabet*. Illustrated by Carol Newsom. New York: Lothrop, Lee & Shepard, 1983.

Munari, Bruno. *Bruno Munari's ABC*. Cleveland: World, 1960.

Wild, Robin and Jocclyn. *The Bears' ABC Book*. New York: J.B. Lippincott, 1972.

Wildsmith, Brian. *Brian Wildsmith's ABC*. New York: Franklin Watts, 1963.

Beginning-to-Read Books

Beginning readers are often directed to the shelves in a library or bookstore containing special types of books called beginning-to-read books. These were written according to formulas which control the difficulty of the book. Beginning-to-read books have
1. a limited number of words,
2. few words on a page,
3. short words,
4. short sentences,
5. large print, and
6. illustrations that give clues to meaning.

These qualities are supposed to make the books easier to read than other picture books. Recent research which identifies elements such as story structure, repetition, and predictability as influential aids to reading would question whether beginning-to-read books are easier for children to read. Many of them are not. Beginning readers should not confine their selection to beginning-to-read books. If they look in the regular picture book section of the library, they will find a number of beautifully written and illustrated books which just happen to be easy to read.

There are two types of good beginning-to-read books—those that were written with controlled vocabulary and just happened to develop into entertaining stories, and those good stories that just happen to be easy to read. In either case, what is important in a beginning-to-read story is that the story itself be entertaining. A list of good beginning-to-read books:

Eastman, P.D. *Go, Dog, Go!* New York: Random House, 1961.
Freschet, Bernice. *Moose Baby.* Illustrated by Jim Pirosky. New York: G.P. Putnam, 1979.
Himler, Ronald. *Wake Up, Jeremiah.* New York: Harper & Row, 1979.
Hutchins, Pat. *Rosie's Walk.* New York: Macmillan, 1968.
——. *Goodnight Owl.* New York: Macmillan, 1972.
Lobel, Arnold. *Owl at Home.* New York: Harper & Row, 1975.
——. *Frog and Toad* (series). New York: Harper & Row, 1970, 1972, 1976.
Minarik, Elsa H. *Little Bear* (series). Illustrated by Maurice Sendak. New York: Harper & Row, 1957.
——. *Cat and Dog.* Illustrated by Fritz Siebel. New York: Harper & Row, 1960.
Seuss, Dr. *Hop on Pop.* New York: Random House, 1963.
——. *One Fish, Two Fish, Red Fish, Blue Fish.* New York: Random House, 1960.
Stadler, John. *Cat at Bat.* New York: E.P. Dutton, 1979.
Tether, Graham. *Skunk and Possum.* Illustrated by Lucinda McQueen. Boston: Houghton Mifflin, 1979.
Wilie, Joanne. *A Big Fish Story.* New York: Children's Press, 1983.

A Reading-Readiness Checklist

Reading readiness is not an accumulation of little behaviors that can be checked off until the child is ready for formal reading instruction. Nevertheless, it is helpful for you to have a list of indicators of progress toward reading. The following list is divided into three areas of readiness: oral language development, book awareness, and concepts of print (which are discovered through both reading and writing activities). Most of the items on the checklist can be identified easily.

Oral Language Development
Can your child make all of the sounds clearly when he or she is talking?
Can your child rhyme words?
Can your child make lists of words that begin with the same sound?
Can your child speak in sentences at least five words long?
Does your child use dependent clauses in sentences?
Does your child have a large oral vocabulary?
Is your child interested in new words?
Can your child tell a story that is familiar?
Can your child make up a story?

Book Awareness
Can your child tell the front from the back of a book?
Can your child tell when the book is right-side-up?
Can your child find the title page?
Does your child know what an author is?
Does your child know what an illustrator is?
Can your child find where the story starts?
Can your child distinguish between print and pictures?
Does your child know where to begin reading on a page?
Does your child know that the left page is read before the right one?
Can your child turn pages correctly as he or she looks at a book?

Turning pages correctly is one characteristic of book awareness.

Can your child point to the direction the print takes, going from left to right across a line and then back to the left again?
Can your child point to individual words as they are read or point to individual words as you count them on a line (visual word boundaries)?
Can your child match a word on a card with the same word on a page of text?
Can your child turn the pages at the appropriate time when a story is being read aloud?
Can your child find a familiar book on a bookshelf?
Can your child tell a story to a simple, wordless picture book?
Does your child pretend to read books?
Does your child look at books independently?

Concepts of Print
Does your child notice words and symbols in the environment—street signs, speed limit signs, logos for familiar stores, newspaper and magazine headlines, recipes, and logos on familiar foods?
Can your child write mock letters (i.e., ∧ ⊏ ϙ ᘔ), mock words, and some familiar words?
Can your child write his or her name legibly?
Does your child invent spellings? Can you read them?
Does your child write, scribble, and create print from left to right on a page?
Does your child write, scribble, and create print from top to bottom on a page?
Does your child return to the left for a second line of print?
Does your child differentiate between an alphabet letter and a word?
Does your child leave spaces or in other ways make distinctions between words in writing?
Is your child eager to write? Does your child choose to write and draw during free time?
Does your child ask a lot of questions about print?
Does your child ask adults to write for him or her?
Can your child pace dictation (talk at a speed where you can write and keep up with the dictation)?
Is your child aware that print always has meaning?

Chapter 2

Reading Aloud with Children

The Reading Mother
—Strickland Gillilan

I had a Mother who read to me
Sagas of pirates who scoured the sea,
Cutlasses clenched in their yellow teeth,
"Prisoners" stowed in the hold beneath.

I had a Mother who read me lays
Of ancient and gallant and golden days;
Stories of Marmion and Ivanhoe,
Which every boy has a right to know.

I had a Mother who read me tales
Of Gelert the hound of the hills of Wales—
True to his trust till his tragic death,
Faithfulness blent with his final breath.

I had a Mother who read me things
That wholesome life to the boy heart brings—
Stories that stir with an upward touch.
Oh, that each mother of boys were such!

You may have tangible wealth untold;
Caskets of jewels and coffers of gold.
Richer than I you can never be—
I had a Mother who read to me.

Reading aloud provides a child with many happy, memorable moments.

Most parents underestimate the powerful impact reading aloud has on their children's development as readers. This chapter will explain why reading aloud is vitally important, provide some suggestions for making reading-aloud sessions effective, and make book recommendations for oral reading.

Why Read Aloud?

Most parents recognize that reading aloud is a happy experience for preschool children, but few realize the powerful impact it has on both preschool and school-age children. Reading aloud has an influence upon children's reading development, their feelings of warmth with regard to their families, their development of curiosity, their knowledge of literature, and their knowledge of information contained in the books that are read.

The foremost reason for reading aloud to your child is that reading aloud brings your family together for happy, memorable moments. I remember my father reading aloud to me every night before bed. We would crawl up on his big double bed, prop up the pillows, and read from a series called *My Book House*. You can imagine my immense pleasure at rediscovering the entire set in my parents' attic and sharing the books with my own daughter!

HI AND LOIS

READ US ANOTHER STORY, DAD

MY EYES ARE TIRED

YOU CAN CLOSE THEM

I CAN'T READ WITH MY EYES CLOSED

WE DON'T CARE ABOUT THE STORY. WE'RE HERE FOR THE CUDDLING

The emotional values of reading aloud far surpass any intellectual gains made by children, astounding as those may be. Reading aloud helps you establish and maintain close communication with your children. One family spent a summer hiking the Appalachian Trail together. Each evening before bed they read aloud from a paperback book they carried along for that purpose. The reading-aloud time became one of the most valued experiences of the hiking adventure—so much so that even after returning home, they continued to provide time each day to read aloud to each other.

We often read in the newspapers about estranged adolescents and hear of parents who "just can't communicate" with their children anymore. Book-sharing can provide regular happy family encounters free from conflicts or confrontations. Books can create a tie that bonds family relationships.

The second most important reason to read aloud with your child is to provide him or her with a foundation for lifetime reading habits. Children have the right to be exposed to interesting, humorous, entertaining, and thought-provoking stories and poems that are a part of our culture. This exposure

Children exposed to a variety of literature soon develop a love of books.

reaps untold benefits by creating a love of literature in your child. The thirst for good books lasts a lifetime.

Annis Duff, author of *Bequest of Wings: A Family's Pleasure with Books* (Viking, 1944), finds the impact of literature on her children to be noticeable. "People often said to us, 'How does it happen that your children know so many books? Mine have never asked for them.' It does not just happen; children seldom do *ask* for books as an initial stage in learning to love them. Reading, for young children, is rarely a pleasure in isolation but comes through shared pleasure and constant, discerning exposure to books so that they fall naturally into the category of pleasant necessities, along with food, sleep, music and all out-of-doors." Dorothy Butler claims that *Babies Need Books* (New York: Atheneum, 1980). She says that "involvement with books from babyhood is one of the greatest blessings and benefits that can come to any child."

The third most important reason to read aloud is to promote your child's intellectual development.

There is much information in the books we read aloud to children that helps them learn about the world, its people, and the way they live. Literature can provide the link between children's direct experiences and those of the world beyond them. The reading of fiction (such as horse novels by Marguerite Henry and Walter Farley) often leads to reading informational books on the same topic.

Toddlers involved with books from babyhood grow into avid lifelong readers.

The last reason to read aloud is the one which is best documented and probably best known. Reading aloud helps children learn how to read and develops advanced reading skills for children who are already readers. How does reading aloud help children learn how to read?

Children are learning from the moment they are born, and reading aloud stimulates their language development. Two researchers found that parents who sang lullabies to their babies while rocking them had closer bonds with their infants and observed them more closely. The singing of the mother elicited cooing and answering sounds from the infant even on the first day of life. In a study of older infants from thirteen to thirty months of age who were systematically read to by their parents, it was shown that they were able to produce more language sounds than a group of children who had not been read to. Other studies of preschool children have determined that those who have been read to since they were infants are those who have superior language abilities.

Reading aloud to preschoolers helps them learn about written language and to become familiar with stories. Children who have been read to by their parents score higher on school readiness tests than children who have not been read to.

Specifically, children who have been read to learn
- that print contains a message that is meaningful;
- that print moves across the page from left to right;
- that books have a front and a back and a top and a bottom;
- that pictures are different from words;
- that the white spaces between the black letters on a page are word boundaries;
- that one can match words in a text to spoken words;
- that stories have a beginning, a middle, and an ending;
- that plots of stories are often predictable.

Many of these concepts may seem obvious but it is amazing how often children are taught how to read before they understand what reading is all about. Reading is not a passive activity where children sit back like empty containers while words fill up their heads with information. Reading is an active reasoning process where children are constantly making predictions about the meaning of written language. Reading

THE FAMILY CIRCUS By Bil Keane

"Where does it say 'To be continued tomorrow night'?"

Youngsters imitate adult models by reading to their dolls and to baby brothers and sisters.

aloud contributes significantly to the development of these reasoning abilities.

Children who have been read to since birth copy the adult model and read to their dolls and to each other. It is quite natural that they become independent readers at an early age.

Children who become early readers have one thing in common with each other: they were read to by their parents or older siblings. In two classic studies, Margaret Clark, author of *Young Fluent Readers,* and Dolores Durkin, who wrote *Children Who Read Early,* discovered that reading aloud was a common background experience shared by early readers. More recently, the same finding has been documented after analyzing a number of other studies of early readers. In some cases, we even know how parents read aloud with early readers, so we can begin to document the specific behaviors that make reading aloud such a powerful influence upon the acquisition of reading ability.

Reading aloud is even more important today than it was years ago because so many recreational opportunities vie for children's time. Television still tends to be the babysitter and passive entertainer for far too many children. Studies show that

Being read to by parents and older siblings encourages children to become early readers.

virtually all children are regular television viewers (averaging over six hours a day) while fewer than half of our children are regular readers. If one-fourth of the time children spend watching television could be spent in reading with family members, we would have a nation of avid readers.

Parents cannot assume that teachers are reading aloud in school. Teachers today are pressed to fit all of the required textbook instruction into the day. One of the first frills to leave the curriculum is reading aloud to the class.

There can be no doubt that reading aloud to children is extremely important. Two books have been published on that topic alone: *For Reading Out Loud!* by Margaret Kimmel and Elizabeth Segel (Delacorte, 1984) and *The Read-Aloud Handbook* by Jim Trelease (New York: Penguin, 1980). The many reasons why reading aloud is invaluable have been cited repeatedly. Yet the most convincing reasons for reading aloud can only be seen by adults practicing the art. Any family activity that is as pleasurable as reading aloud deserves a high priority in homes and schools.

General Guidelines

There are techniques for reading aloud that vary according to the age of the child, but there are also some general points that apply when reading to children of all ages.

Read books that you yourself enjoy. If possible, preview the books. Read reviews when deciding what books to buy or to borrow from the library. Reviews can be found occasionally in national newspapers and newsmagazines, in professional educational journals, in newsletters and magazines for parents, and in books devoted to suggesting good read-aloud children's books. A list of recommended books is found in Chapter 8. No matter how highly recommended a book is, though, unless you yourself are enthusiastic about it, the read-aloud session will not be effective.

Stop reading a book when either your interest or the interest of the child or children wanes. Read-aloud sessions for babies might be extremely short if their attention is not focused on the book. Older children need to know that when the reading is not entertaining or interesting to them, it can be brought to an end. Some books are far more appropriate for independent reading; far fewer make good read-aloud books. And children's interests change from time to time. After a long string of science fiction, children may prefer another type of book.

Good lighting and comfort are important ingredients of the read-aloud session.

Growing Up Reading

Find a comfortable spot for reading aloud. Places that are suitable offer good lighting. Beds are the most popular spot for reading aloud, especially if the sessions are a part of the bedtime routine. Children enjoy climbing up on their parents' bed for a special treat. Sofas, rocking chairs, pillows, bean bag chairs, and a shady spot under a tree are some favorite places to read. And, of course, many families read on trips, in the car, and in waiting rooms. It is important that both you and the children are comfortable and can see the book's text clearly.

Many families take along books to read while traveling.

Read at routine times. Reading habits only become habits when they become a part of daily routines. Certain times of the day are best for some people. Sessions usually go better when both the reader and the children are relaxed, calm, and quiet. Reading when you are thinking about something else, such as what needs to be done during the day, is rarely entertaining. Sometimes mothers and fathers have different routines. Or, they alternate: when Dad finishes one book, Mother begins another and the whole family (including the parent not reading) is entertained.

Put expression into your reading. Expression can be over-dramatic, but more oral readers tend to be monotonous rather than dramatic. Children of all ages enjoy a bit of the dramatic in story reading. The purpose of the reading is entertainment, not education.

Be responsive to your child's reaction. As Kimmel and Segel state in *For Reading Out Loud!* reading aloud is a performance—its quality improves when you are really interacting with your audience.

Allow time for children to settle into a story. Give them advance notice that you are about to read and, with children who are old enough to respond, you might ask a question to orient them to the reading that is to come.

Allow time after reading for discussion. Refrain from questions such as "Did you like that story?" because the child is likely to simply say yes and stop thinking about it. Ask questions that stimulate thought; share opinions. Some books arouse emotions or ideas that need to be dealt with after reading. Avoid turning post-reading times into quizzes about the book, however.

Adjust your reading pace to fit your story and the children in your audience. In *The Read-Aloud Handbook* Jim Trelease claims that the most frequent mistake adults make in oral reading is going too fast. Give the children you are reading to time to really think about what you are reading.

Arrange to have the books that you read aloud available for a few days afterward so that the child or children can return to them for silent reading and rereading.

Extend the book. Either pick books on topics of interest to your children or involve them in related activities while you are reading the stories. Purchase some pumpernickel bread while reading *Pumpernickel Tickle and Mean Green Cheese* by Nancy Patz, for example.

Encourage children's participation in the reading session. In good read-aloud sessions, infants are pointing and chanting with the reader, toddlers are supplying missing words from picture cues, prereaders are memorizing and repeating texts, beginning readers are beginning to read bits of the text, and mature readers are taking turns in the actual reading. At appropriate places in the texts children are asking questions, making comments, and anticipating what will happen next. Oral reading sessions are by no means a one-way flow of language.

Allow no interruptions while reading aloud unless there is an

Toddlers can participate by pointing to pictures and saying words together.

emergency. If the phone rings, tell the caller you will return the call just as soon as the story is over.

Age-Specific Guidelines

In addition to these general guidelines, you will want to think about some specific reading behaviors that are especially appropriate for children of different ages.

Infants

While reading to infants, it is important to be responsive to the child's physical movements. Make sure the baby is comfortable. Be responsive to your baby's interest as well. Instead of reading from the beginning to the end of a book, watch where the child is looking, and read or talk about that part. If your child starts to look away or wiggle, the session should terminate. If your infant is teething, it is wise to provide a teething toy so that he or she is not encouraged to put the book into the mouth. Encourage page turning if the book has cardboard pages. If you keep all of the pages in your hand except the next one to be turned, the infant will be able to turn a page easily.

Pointing to things in pictures and labeling them orally is especially important in the first year when your infant, though not yet talking, is acquiring so much language. Relate what is in the book to your infant's experience. "You have a ball just like that one!" Repetition is important also. After seeing a page several times, your infant will begin to recognize the pictures. You'll quickly come to realize your infant has distinct book preferences.

The last guideline is: The earlier you begin to read aloud, the better. If your child can become used to having stories read aloud before he or she starts walking, reading-aloud sessions can be sustained during those mobile, early walking times. Children who are learning to walk have a hard time sitting still to listen to a story if they have not previously become hooked on book reading.

Toddlers

Toddler reading sessions can also be extremely short. Your toddler will enjoy carrying small books around the house. But he or she is likely to rapidly lose interest and go trotting away while

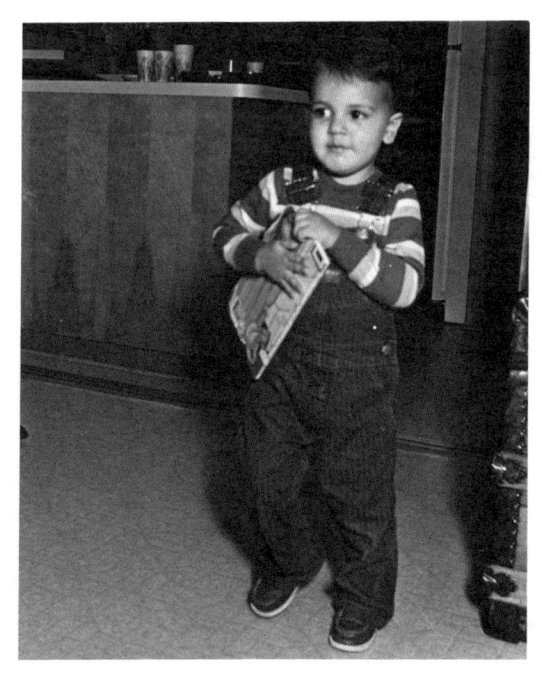

Toddler reading sessions should be short, or your audience may wander off—book and all!

Growing Up Reading

you are reading. You may find it helpful to read aloud when your child is sleepy, either just before or just after a nap, and at bedtime. Have alternative books available in case the first one you choose is rejected. (Toddlers *love* to say *no!*)

Pointing out things in pictures and encouraging your toddler to participate in the "reading" helps your child become more active in the reading process. Maybe you have tried to skip a page or shorten a story in an effort to speed up the bedtime ritual. Has your toddler surprised you by noticing and demanding the whole story? Even at these young ages, toddlers are actively listening to stories and remembering them word for word!

Because reading sessions with your toddler are likely to be so short, it is important to read aloud frequently—several times during the day. There are natural breaks in the day, so it is helpful to carry books in your purse or a bookbag so that they are handy when needed—in waiting rooms, traffic snarls, restaurants, and the like. At home reading aloud makes a nice short break from housework. One mom I know reads to her toddler during lunch! If you store books in boxes in several

Leaving books within easy reach will result in spontaneous read-aloud sessions.

different rooms in your house, reading aloud is more likely to pop up spontaneously.

Preschoolers
Your preschooler presents a special challenge because the way that you read to him or her influences his or her reading readiness. Preschoolers request favorite stories over and over

Preschoolers learn about word boundaries as you point to words that are being read.

again. One day I overheard a child plead with his mother to take *Curious George* out of the library. The mother replied, "No, you have already read that book." How tragic, for it is by reading favorite stories over and over again that children are able to memorize the stories. That is the first step in becoming an independent reader. The books that have been read aloud should be available afterwards for independent reading. Your child will be able to turn the pages at the appropriate places when you are reading and to retell stories in his own words. If you provide a flannel board, puppets, or props, you may hear many different versions of a story!

Point to the words as you read. Sweep your finger along from left to right and then back again, and point to specific key words, such as the names of the characters. Pointing helps the child learn the mechanics of reading. As children are nearing the time they begin to read, they need to know that the white spaces between words mark the boundaries of words. This can be done by pointing to each individual word separately in a text which has few words on a page and a fair amount of white space between the words. Of course, pointing can be overdone and it can turn read-aloud sessions into direct reading lessons, and that would be a shame. Reading to children, especially preschoolers, should be primarily for entertainment.

It is fun to tape-record your preschooler's rendition of a story and let the child hear the tape. Since picture books are typically rather short and since preschoolers can often sustain long periods for reading aloud, most sessions will involve reading more than one book. You'll want to make frequent visits to the library to sustain the read-aloud sessions with new and fresh material as well as the old favorites.

Primary Grade Children
Children beginning to read by themselves enjoy sharing in the read-aloud sessions. They love an audience for their new-found skill. Yet, because they read so slowly, they often tire easily, making the session less entertaining and enjoyable in the long run. One suggestion is to assist your children in reading aloud by taking turns. You become a model for reading when you read, and your child doesn't get tired from reading too much. Although your beginning reader might be able to make it all the way through an easy-to-read book, it would be a difficult task. Alternating pages or even sentences with your child can often sustain rather long periods of oral reading.

Beginning readers enjoy being recorded. Your child might enjoy listening to tapes of stories and following along in the texts. You can borrow cassettes from your local library or purchase them from Weston Woods, Weston, CT 06883. Beginning readers should not be limited to beginning-to-read books, most of which have been written in less exciting language styles than typical picture books. Beginning readers need the stimulation of other, more advanced books being read to them. Encourage your child to read the same story over again

Beginning readers enjoy listening to tapes and following along in the text.

until his or her oral reading becomes fluent rather than just a word-for-word reading. If your child makes a mistake while reading, ignore that mistake unless it alters substantially the meaning of the text. Then ask, "Does that make sense? Want to try it again?" The child may correct his or her own mistake if allowed to do so. Fledgling readers do not profit from criticism, no matter how well intended it is.

Often when children learn to read for themselves, parents stop reading aloud to them. This is sad, for no matter how well we read, we can still enjoy the oral tradition of children's literature. Reading aloud is not merely for the purpose of helping children learn how to read. It is also to help youngsters develop the reading habit and to reinforce close family communication and relationships.

Mature Readers
Mature readers enjoy hearing books that would be especially difficult for them to read alone—books with dialect, with advanced vocabulary, or written years ago with less familiar

language. Longer books which would take a long time to read independently can be sustained in family reading sessions. Read-aloud sessions for mature readers are pure family entertainment. You can get a bit dramatic in reading aloud. You'll enjoy subtle nuances of vocal inflections, oral interpretations, and performance strategies at this more advanced level of oral reading.

Reading aloud is a lifetime activity. Even high school

For older readers, reading aloud can be pure entertainment.

students and adults enjoy sharing a good book. Cassettes of Great Books for Children can be ordered from The Mind's Eye, Box 6727, San Francisco, CA 94101.

Group Reading
Many families have more than one child. Reading aloud to a group of two or more children can bring a special challenge. It is akin in some ways to reading aloud to a group in school. If the children are close together in age, one story is likely to be equally entertaining to both of them. When babies are tiny, however, it is not likely that equal amounts of attention can be focused on

two different children. If you have young children, you'll need to plan separate and group read-aloud times. Your older children will enjoy reading aloud to their younger siblings.

Once the youngest child has turned five (or can sit for longer periods to enjoy literature), books that will appeal to all ages can be shared. Some picture books are appealing to older children and adults. They have outstanding illustrations or stories that are humorous or thoughtful. Some poetry picture collections and larger books appeal to all ages.

In multi-age group settings it helps to have periodic eye contact with each child personally. Group reading sessions often terminate in better discussions or related activities than sessions with just one child.

Books for Reading Aloud

Some types of literature are meant to be read or told out loud. They do not read as well silently as they do orally. Poetry, humor, and the traditional folktales make ideal read-aloud material. Some nonfiction, which may be difficult reading for children, is good to read aloud to broaden children's experiences with books.

It is important at every age level for children to experience a variety of literature so that when they get tired of a particular type of book there are alternatives. Some types of literature are particularly appropriate for particular ages of children.

Infants
Point-and-say books have pictures of familiar objects and little text. The object of reading this type of literature is to increase your child's vocabulary, to compare pictures in a book with known items in the environment, to familiarize the child with books, and to show your baby that books have meaning.

Nursery rhymes, chants, poems, and songs are best chanted or sung throughout the day rather than just presented at read-aloud sessions. Then, at a later time, it can be thrilling to watch your infant associate the rhymes that he or she already knows with the picture representing that rhyme in a book. Nursery rhymes help your child become familiar with the sounds of language. They assist the transition from telegraphic

Point-and-say books help increase a young child's vocabulary.

speech, where one word represents a sentence, to mature language, where each word is pronounced.

Participation books are popular with older infants. These are books like Dorothy Kunhardt's popular *Pat the Bunny* (Western Publishing, Co., Inc. 1940, 1968) which your child can manipulate. Babies enjoy different textures, pages with holes in them, and books to explore safely, by touching. Cardboard books are especially good for infants who are teething.

You can make participation books out of cardboard, fabric scraps, and other textured surfaces. These are like toys for your baby, but because they have a book format, they introduce your child to books. Homemade storybooks, usually illustrated with photographs of the baby, become favorites as well. You can make a point-and-say book by using pictures cut out of magazines.

Toddlers
Your toddler will enjoy the classic fairy tales read over and over again. Stories like *The Three Little Pigs* or *The Three Billy Goats Gruff*

will encourage your child to chant the repetitive parts as he or she sings and plays around the house. You and your toddler can act out the tales. If you make a flannel board with characters of these familiar stories or have puppets for the story characters, your child can experience the stories in lots of ways other than just by hearing them. Active involvement in the story plot is a real key for toddlers.

Your toddler will enjoy books that are small in size because they are easy to carry around the house. Harper & Row's *Nutshell Library* collections have been popular for some time. But there are many new collections using the works of Maurice Sendak, Jean de Brunoff, and other popular children's authors.

Your toddler will still enjoy much of the literature that appealed to him or her as an infant—nursery rhymes especially. Some toddlers can proceed through a favorite Mother Goose collection and chant each rhyme.

Your toddler will also enjoy bigger books which are "two laps wide" for lap reading. Many children's picture books are wider than they are long so that you can spread the book out and see the pictures. *The Very Hungry Caterpillar* by Eric Carle is a book which has manipulative pages as well. It is a most popular toddler read-aloud book.

Toddlers are captivated by big, wide picture books with colorful illustrations.

Books with bright illustrations are especially appropriate for toddlers who are "reading" the pictures, rather than the words. Colorful illustrations by such artists as Eric Carle, Brian Wildsmith, and Gyo Fujikawa are perfect.

At the age of the "terrible twos" your toddler will learn that one way to acquire positive attention is to carry a book up to you and ask to be read to. Your two-year-old has discovered "favorite" books, which need to be read frequently.

Preschoolers
The picture book is a favorite for preschoolers. There are so many different types, sizes, and shapes of picture books that it is hard to classify them. Since the prime ingredient for reading aloud at this age is repetition, books that are easy to repeat and memorize need to be selected. Examples include fairy tales and folktales which have predictable plots, song picture books, rhyming poems which are easily memorized because of their rhyming sounds, stories with repetition in them, and short stories with few words on a page that can be memorized with the help of picture cues.

One of the first things that attracts your preschooler to a picture book is its illustrations. The pictures often keep children's attention while they are being read to. How important it is, then, to give your child the most beautifully illustrated books! Children learn to appreciate a variety of art media: paintings, woodcuts, prints, photographs, sketches, and collages. You can integrate the study of art into your read-aloud sessions by planning a series of sessions using books by the same illustrator or books with the same type of illustration.

There are a number of book clubs on the market that will supply you with a new book for your child each month. In most clubs the books are the same types of books, often by the same author. Your preschool child needs variety and quality in the literature read to him. Because there are so many picture books available, many are of poor quality. Their illustrations are not beautiful or their texts are boring. It is helpful, therefore, to read book recommendations and to ask librarians for suggestions for good read-aloud books for this age group. It also helps to preview books that you are going to read aloud so that you eliminate those which you know ahead of time will not be successful.

Your preschooler will enjoy some of the wordless picture books that have been published in recent years. Some of these, however, are a bit too complicated for preschoolers and have more appeal to older children. Many ABC and counting books are perfect for preschoolers.

Primary Grade Children

Many of the books that are written for the beginning reader are not good for reading aloud. Books with controlled vocabulary, short choppy sentences, and simple plots may be good for beginning readers who are practicing their skills but they are boring for oral reading. When your child is just learning to read, he or she needs to hear how you use expression when reading aloud—how you phrase things and use punctuation as clues for pauses and emphasis—and how you read fluently. The best books for reading out loud are picture storybooks.

Books are easier to read if they have been heard repeatedly. Your child will like having familiar stories read over and over when he is just learning to read. Select books with few words on a page and picture cues to the text. Such books will be the first that your beginning reader will be able to read independently.

Your child will still enjoy having you read aloud even after he has learned to read. Choose some stories that your child cannot read independently yet. Such books include longer picture books and books with chapters in them and fewer illustrations.

Chapter-a-day books make excellent bedtime reading, reinforcing the reading habit. Some chapter-a-day books that are especially suitable for younger children include: *The Wizard of Oz, Ozma of Oz,* and other *Oz* books by L. Frank Baum; *Charlotte's Web* by E. B. White; Marguerite Henry's horse stories, including *Misty of Chincoteague* and *Stormy, Misty's Foal;* Eleanor Estes's books about the Pye family including *Ginger Pye* and *Pinky Pye;* Carolyn Haywood's stories about Betsy and Eddie, including *B is for Betsy; Mr. Popper's Penguins* by Richard and Florence Atwater; and books by Beverly Cleary.

Books that make it easy to take turns reading are ideal for

reading aloud with your beginning reader. These include books with little print on each page so that alternating the reading of pages does not tire your child. Plays are another excellent type of book to share with a beginning reader. Each person takes one or more parts and reads only his or her lines in the play.

Mature Readers
Even mature readers can benefit from having books read to them when the books are harder than the ones they might read themselves.

Older children enjoy books with longer chapters and more complex plots. Science fiction is a wonderful type of literature to read aloud. Adventure stories with a good bit of suspense, and even good mysteries, make excellent read-aloud literature for mature readers.

Specialized science books with technical terminology are another type of book that can be shared orally because they are hard to read, even for a mature reader.

Some classic stories for mature readers include *Treasure Island, Robin Hood, The Hobbit, The Adventures of Tom Sawyer,* and *The Incredible Journey.*

Reading to older children helps them appreciate books that would be difficult for them to read on their own.

Multi-Aged Groups

Groups with both older and younger children in them enjoy picture books if their illustrations are remarkably beautiful and the text is not babyish. Examples of picture books which appeal to all ages include: *I Stood Upon a Mountain* by Aileen Fisher, *The Ox-Cart Man* by Donald Hall, and *A Peaceable Kingdom: The Shaker Abecedarius* by Alice and Martin Provensen. Humorous books often appeal to all ages. Bill Peet's stories and books such as *"Stand Back," Said the Elephant*, *"I'm Going to Sneeze"* are popular.

In *For Reading Out Loud!* Kimmel and Segel list the following books as appealing to a wide age range and therefore as being ideal for family reading:

Arkin, Alan. *The Lemming Condition.* Illustrated by Joan Sandin. New York: Harper & Row, 1976; Bantam Books, 1977.

Babbitt, Natalie. *Tuck Everlasting.* New York: Farrar, Straus & Giroux, 1975; Bantam Books, 1976.

Burnford, Sheila. *The Incredible Journey.* Boston: Little, Brown and Company, 1961; Bantam Books, 1981.

Byars, Betsy. *The House of Wings.* Illustrated by Daniel Schwartz. New York: The Viking Press, 1972; Penguin, Puffin Books, 1982.

Cleary, Beverly. *Ramona the Pest.* Illustrated by Louis Darling. New York: William Morrow & Company, 1968; Dell, 1982.

Cresswell, Helen. *The Piemakers*. Illustrated by Judith Gwyn Brown. New York: Macmillan, 1967.

Dahl, Roald. *Fantastic Mr. Fox*. Illustrated by Donald Chaffin. New York: Alfred A. Knopf, 1970; Bantam Books, 1978.

Fitzgerald, John D. *The Great Brain*. Illustrated by Mercer Mayer. New York: The Dial Press, 1967; Dell, 1977.

Fleischman, Sid. *By the Great Horn Spoon!*. Illustrated by Eric Von Schmidt. Boston: Little, Brown and Company, 1963.

Gilbreth, Frank B. and Ernestine G. Carey. *Cheaper by the Dozen*. New York: Thomas Y. Crowell, 1948; Bantam Books, 1981.

Godden, Rumer. *The Mousewife*. Illustrated by Heidi Holder. New York: The Viking Press, 1982.

Grahame, Kenneth. *The Wind in the Willows*. 1908. Illustrated by Ernest H. Shepard. New York: Charles Scribner's Sons, 1933. (Paperback: many publishers.)

Hale, Lucretta P. *The Complete Peterkin Papers*. 1880. Boston: Houghton Mifflin, 1960; Dover Publications, 1960.

Jarrell, Randall. *The Animal Family*. Illustrated by Maurice Sendak. New York: Pantheon Books, 1965.

Kipling, Rudyard. *Just So Stories*. 1902. Many publishers.

Lester, Julius. *The Knee-High Man and Other Tales*. Illustrated by Ralph Pinto. New York: The Dial Press, 1972.

Lewis, C. S. *The Lion, the Witch and the Wardrobe*. Illustrated by Pauline Baynes. New York: Macmillan, 1951; Macmillan, 1970.

Mowat, Farley. *Owls in the Family*. Illustrated by Robert Frankenberg. Boston: Atlantic-Little, Brown, 1961.

O'Connell, Jean S. *The Dollhouse Caper*. Illustrated by Erik Blegrad. New York: Thomas Y. Crowell, 1976; Scholastic, 1977.

Phelps, Ethel Johnston, editor. *Tatterhood and Other Tales*. Illustrated by Pamela Baldwin Ford. Old Westbury, NY: The Feminist Press, 1978.

Rockwell, Thomas. *How to Eat Fried Worms*. Illustrated by Emily McCully. New York: Franklin Watts, 1973; Dell, 1975.

Sandburg, Carl. *Rootabaga Stories*. 1922. Many publishers.

Sharp, Margery. *The Rescuers*. Illustrated by Garth Williams. Boston: Little Brown and Company, 1959; Dell, 1981.

Singer, Isaac Bashevis. *Zlateh the Goat and Other Stories*. Translated from the Yiddish by the author and Elizabeth Shub. Illustrated by Maurice Sendak. New York: Harper & Row, 1966.

Steig, William. *Abel's Island.* New York: Farrar, Straus & Giroux, 1976; Bantam Books, 1977, 1981.

Thurber, James. *Many Moons.* Illustrated by Louis Slobodkin. New York: Harcourt Brace and World, 1943; Harcourt Brace Jovanovich, 1978.

Tolkien, J. R. R. *The Hobbit or There and Back Again.* rev. ed. New York: Houghton Mifflin Company, 1937, 1938, and 1966; Ballantine Books, 1965.

Twain, Mark. *The Adventures of Tom Sawyer.* 1876. Many publishers.

White, E. B. *Charlotte's Web.* Illustrated by Garth Williams. New York: Harper & Brothers, 1952; Harper & Row, 1974.

Since finding the right book at the right time is a time-consuming process, it helps to acquire a collection of good books that can be used when one does not have time to exchange books at the library or money to purchase new books at the bookstore. I'd recommend a collection such as *My Book House, Childcraft,* or the *Arbuthnot Anthology of Children's Literature.* The advantage of a well-done anthology or collection is that screening has been done to eliminate the poorest stories and poems from the collection. What remains is the best in children's literature, at least at the time the collection was published.

References on Reading Aloud

Berg, Lela. *Reading and Loving.* Exeter, New Hampshire: Heinemann, 1976.

Butler, Dorothy. *Babies Need Books.* New York: Atheneum, 1980.

Butler, Dorothy and Marie Clay. *Reading Begins at Home.* Exeter, New Hampshire: Heinemann, 1979.

Clark, Margaret M. *Young Fluent Readers.* Exeter, New Hampshire: Heinemann, 1976.

Duff, Annis. *Bequest of Wings: A Family's Pleasure with Books.* New York: Viking, 1944.

Durkin, Dolores. *Children Who Read Early.* New York: Teachers College Press, 1966.

Hearne, Betsy. *Choosing Books for Children: A Commonsense Guide.* New York: Delacorte Press, 1981.

Lamme, Linda Leonard, with Vivian Cox, Jane Matanzo, and Miken Olson. *Raising Readers: A Guide to Sharing Literature with Young Children.* New York: Walker and Company, 1980.

Larrick, Nancy. *Children's Reading Begins at Home.* Winston-Salem, North Carolina: Starstream Products, 1980.

A Parent's Guide to Children's Reading. 4th ed. New York: Doubleday, Bantam Books, 1975.

Trelease, Jim. *The Read-Aloud Handbook.* New York: Penguin, 1980.

Chapter 3

Reading Comprehension

"Hey, Mom, what's a procession?"
"Now I get it! The gardener is a bad guy, really!"
"Just to the end of the chapter, please? I'm right in the middle of a sad part!"

Children are really reading only when they are understanding, at least to a degree, the message that an author has written down. Reading is an active process. Children use the wide range of experiences they have had to interpret what an

THE FAMILY CIRCUS By Bil Keane

"I like reading. It turns on a picture in your head."

author has written. If they read enough (or are read to enough), children predict what is going to happen in stories. They question the author as they read. They are actively involved in matching their expectations with what is written on the page.

Levels of Comprehension

There are many levels at which your child can comprehend a story. The first level is *memory*. Gradually, your child is able to remember more and more about the story until he has memorized it down to the tiniest detail. This lowest level of comprehension is called the *literal* level. The literal level is important because it occurs so frequently in our lives. We need to comprehend at literal levels to remember phone numbers,

Remembering phone numbers, addresses, and directions requires literal comprehension.

addresses, or directions. When cooking, an accurate reading of recipes is vital. When sewing, the pattern must be followed precisely. Repair manuals, road maps, coupons, and construction kits are some of the materials we must comprehend literally. Hardly a day goes by when we don't use literal comprehension to understand memos, street signs, contents of food containers, and other writing in our environment. If we concentrate only on the literal level of comprehension, however, we do our children a disservice. Higher levels of comprehension may not occur so frequently, but their uses can be critically important.

A second level of comprehension is the *inferential level*. At this level you do more than merely recall what you've read: You make interpretations. Inferential comprehension includes recognizing cause-and-effect relationships, finding main ideas, making comparisons, describing characters, predicting outcomes, interpreting figurative language, analyzing details, and generalizing beyond the reading material itself. In contrast to the literal level—where you are merely remembering what is read—at the inferential level, you're thinking about the content. Most of the reading we do for fun or information is done at the inferential level. We compare the views of columnists, laugh at comic strips, and interpret sports scores in daily newspapers. We cry (if we are sentimental) or otherwise react to the novels we read. Letters we receive in the mail usually require interpretation. If we read only at the literal level, we would be depriving ourselves of our enjoyment of literature and of thoughtful interaction with writing of many types.

The most complex level of comprehension is called *critical comprehension*. At this level you give opinions based upon criteria to determine the quality of the material. Areas of comprehension at the critical level include distinguishing reality from fantasy, discriminating between fact and opinion, valuing, finding propaganda techniques, and judging the overall quality of books. Critical readers are selective about the authors they pursue. They seek out works by familiar authors. They reject poorly written works. Critical comprehension is essential in a literate, democratic society. Poor readers believe everything they read. Good readers take note of the sources of information. We all need to read campaign literature critically prior to voting. We decide what products to purchase based upon advertising, product reviews, and labeling. Critical comprehension allows us to make decisions about our lives based upon what we read. How important it is, then, that children learn to read critically!

These levels of comprehension are not necessarily sequential. That is, readers do not need to be able to comprehend literally before they learn inferential skills. Rather, these

Critical comprehension skills help a reader make decisions and choose between products of different quality.

comprehension levels serve to focus our attention on some types of thinking which are part of reading comprehension.

Comprehension Strategies

How can you help your child develop his or her reading comprehension? The more your child reads, the more practice he or she is getting at comprehending. Different reading materials provide practice in different areas of comprehension, and the questions you ask can influence your child's comprehension.

A child need not be able to read in order to develop comprehension strategies. Children practice their comprehension strategies through listening as well as through reading.

Growing Up Reading

As was mentioned in Chapter 2, it is important to read aloud to your child at levels beyond what he is capable of reading himself.

Main Idea

Your child should be able to recall the main idea from a passage he has read. You can read a story without the pictures to very young children and then help them match the picture on the cover of the book to the title that they have heard read aloud. Making captions for pictures helps older children get the main idea of a picture. Children of all ages enjoy creating interesting captions for colorful photographs. One way to test main-idea comprehension is to give your child three topic choices and have him or her select which one is the main idea of a given paragraph.

Reading the comics helps a child distinguish between the main idea and less important ideas.

Newspapers are great sources of reading exercise. Help your child get the main idea of jokes and comics. Have your child read news stories with the headline covered up. Compare your homemade headlines with those in the paper.

A topic sentence is usually the first one in a paragraph. Read only the first sentence, and then have your child guess what the paragraph will be about.

In addition to writing captions for pictures, your child can create titles for poems, comic strips, and other forms of writing. Short selections are best for practicing getting the main idea.

After your child has read a book, encourage him to think about who else might like to read it. Ask your child to tell you about the book.

If the child can easily tell you in a sentence or two about the book or article, he or she has understood the main idea. If it takes more talk, your child is still absorbed in details and cannot grasp the main idea.

Sequence and Details

As adults, it is important that we comprehend the details in some of our reading: leases, contracts, directions, and recipes, for example. When reading for pleasure we gloss over details. Your child needs to read for details when looking up information for a report or project, when reading directions to make something, when he or she will be retelling the story, and when seeking answers to very specific questions. Your child is far more likely to notice the details if he or she is actually going to construct a birdhouse than if just reading about birdhouse construction.

Repetition is another way to master details, especially of story sequence. Some stories have matching records or tapes to accompany them so that your child can listen to the story over and over again. Two excellent sources of records and tapes are: Weston Woods, Weston, CT 06883, and Scholastic, Inc., P.O. Box 7502, Jefferson City, MO 65102.

Chapter 1 mentions providing props for acting out the story or using flannel-board characters or puppets as excellent readiness activities. These activities are also reading comprehension exercises. You can tell how well your child is comprehending stories by listening to the stories he or she retells in his or her play. Are all of the characters mentioned? Is the plot sequence complete and correct? Is dialogue used where appropriate? Does the story make sense? Does the story "hang together"?

As your child reads and retells stories, he or she develops what is called a "story schema." This schema is a list of elements found in most stories. For example, children's stories usually begin by describing the setting and introducing the characters. The plot develops until there is a crisis or climax of some sort, after which the problem is solved. In most children's stories, everyone lives "happily ever after." As your child reads such stories many times, he or she becomes aware of this overall story pattern. Then, when your child approaches a new story, he or she will have more accurate predictions about how the new story will evolve. Folktales and fairy tales, which have highly predictable plots, are the best stories for developing a story schema.

Cause and Effect
Another comprehension skill is identifying cause and effect. After reading a passage, ask your child questions about why specific events took place as they did. Can the child trace effects or results to their logical causes? Can he or she imagine or explain what results might occur? Then finish reading to discover the real outcome of the story.

Young children often ask "why" questions. Applying that same curiosity to reading allows your child to improve reading comprehension. Cause-and-effect reasoning becomes much more tangible when children follow directions for assembling something with their parents.

Fact or Opinion?
Recognition of fact and opinion is related to cause-and-effect types of reasoning. Comparing editorials and political cartoons with news reports provides vivid contrasts between fact and opinion. Help your child learn to figure out which facts help support his or her opinions. Together, you can enjoy reading and analyzing people's opinions in the "Letters to the Editor" section of your local newspaper.

Reality or Fantasy?
Young children, particularly, need to be able to distinguish between reality and fantasy. Since so many of the animals in books talk, it is reasonable to assume that at first young children believe that animals can talk. After reading folktales or fairy

tales, it is important to clarify that the story is "just pretend." Help your child investigate real characters and imaginary ones, such as ghosts, trolls, wizards, fairies, elves, leprechauns, and animals with human attributes.

Your child will enjoy studying the history of characters associated with holidays—the Easter Bunny, Santa Claus, St. Valentine. Modern popular art and media have perpetrated a new series of fictionalized beings—Garfield, E.T., Smurfs, Pac-Man, Care Bears, and the like. Many of these characters take on an aura of reality, similar to stuffed animals or toys that are the props for fantasy play with children. One way to help your child distinguish between reality and fantasy is to encourage fantasy play. Children who have rich experiences in pretend play are better able to clearly identify fantasy in books. They recognize the distinction between their own pretend play and reality and can apply that recognition to stories.

Predicting Outcomes
Good readers constantly question an author's assumptions. They actively predict how events in the story will be resolved. Encourage your child to be an active, questioning reader and not to accept passively whatever is read. When you are reading an adventure story aloud or a story with a bit of suspense in it, stop for a moment at the climax and ask your child to predict what the ending might be.

Children's moral development rests upon their abilities to see the perspectives of others who are making decisions about how to behave in certain situations. Reading books with moral dilemmas in them and stopping and deciding what the character "ought" to do will help your child develop moral reasoning skills and reading comprehension skills as well. Ask if the characters should share before reading the endings of these books:

The Mannerly Adventures of Mistress Mouse by Martha Keenan (New York: Crown, 1977.)

Rachel and Obadiah by Brinton Turkle (New York: E.P. Dutton, 1978.)

Morris' Disappearing Bag by Rosemary Wells (New York: Dial, 1979.)

Pet Show by Ezra Jack Keats (New York: Macmillan, 1972.)

Peter's Chair by Ezra Jack Keats (New York: Harper, 1967.)
The Little Red Hen by Paul Galdone (New York: Seabury, 1973.)

Comparison
Find different reading materials dealing with the same topic so there will be opportunities for comparison. Discuss with your child how book characters compare: Winnie-the-Pooh and Paddington, Black Beauty and Black Gold, Tom Sawyer and Huck Finn, and Homer Price and Henry Huggins. Books can be compared: *Wind in the Willows* and *Rabbit Hill, Lassie* and *The Incredible Journey,* and *The Little Engine That Could* and *Little Toot.* Sometimes it is interesting to compare the writings of two authors: Lloyd Alexander and Madeleine L'Engle, or Carolyn Haywood and Beverly Cleary.

Different versions of the same story provide a child with many opportunities for making comparisons.

Find two different versions of the same story. See if your child can detect differences and similarities between them. There are many versions of folktales, fables, nursery rhymes, and fairy tales. Several song picture books have two or more versions for comparison as well:
                    The Farmer in the Dell
         Yankee Doodle   Hush, Little Baby

Evaluation

Book-sharing has become ingrained in our culture. Magazines, Great Book programs, Junior Great Book programs, and discussion groups are a few avenues that offer opportunities for book-sharing.

A friend serves lemonade and cookies on Saturday mornings to her "Literary Club" of neighborhood children who come to share the books that they have read that week. Other than the refreshments, there is no incentive to come—no points awarded for book reading, no stars or stickers or other tangible rewards. But the children seldom miss their Saturday club meetings. Essentially, their book-sharing consists of recommending books to each other. They compare books by the same and different authors and get excited when they find treasure books—books that they want to own and keep forever.

Families can set aside time for book-sharing. Sharing is one way to monitor your child's reading, at least to a degree. Children pick up misconceptions from books if they never discuss them with others.

A more important reason for book-sharing, however, is that it helps your child learn to evaluate books. Young children call all books "good." They soon develop favorites, however. Children learn to be very discriminating readers if you discuss with them what they like best about the stories they read.

Appreciation

The best test of how well children are comprehending what they read is to observe their reaction to books. Children who beg to read "just to the end of the chapter" are so engrossed in their reading that they don't want to put the book down. There is no doubt that they are comprehending what they are reading.

Another indication of comprehension is an emotional response to the story. The child who gets angry in response to an editorial, who weeps during a sad moment in a story, or who chuckles at humor is undoubtedly understanding what he or she is reading. Children who become so engrossed in a book that they are unaware of things going on around them are comprehending what they are reading.

If your child seeks out books by authors he or she has read

previously, the child has, obviously, enjoyed that author's works. A clear sign of comprehension is asking librarians for a book "just like" one already read. Children also enjoy returning to favorite books and rereading them, in the same way they

Asking for another book by the same author, or with a similar theme, shows that a child comprehends what she reads.

enjoy seeing a favorite movie over and over again. At each rereading, a child is probably comprehending at a level that is a bit more sophisticated. He or she will skip or skim parts that are not particularly satisfying and dawdle over the especially enjoyable parts of the story. Purchase books your child especially enjoys so they are available for rereading. Provide subscriptions to magazines your child has enjoyed reading.

There is no doubt that appreciation of literature is really the highest level of reading comprehension. The goal of reading, instruction is to encourage avid reading. Avid readers do not need to be checked on comprehension. Their behaviors reveal far more about comprehension than tests and scores will.

Parental Concerns

Don't worry if your child is reading difficult books that he or she cannot comprehend completely. Adults comprehend car manuals in a different way than they do magazine articles and novels. Children, similarly, seek out easy books, hard books, short stories, long ones, and a variety of literature. They will not completely understand all the books they select. This is fine.

An eight-year-old boy, who was reading the second book in J.R.R. Tolkien's *The Lord of the Rings* trilogy, looked up and sighed contentedly, "Oh, I just love to read books that I almost understand!" Just how this child came to read the trilogy is an interesting story in itself. His mother, tiring of waiting at the table while her two sons (ages eight and twelve) dawdled over their dinner at night, decided to read aloud some books to them while they finished their meals. The first book she selected was *The Hobbit,* which immediately became a favorite. The eight-year-old, having been introduced to Tolkien, just had to have more. After he had plowed his way through all three books in the trilogy, he informed his mom one day that he was going to write a trilogy and left for his room with a pencil in hand. When she checked on him half an hour later, he was found staring into space. He asked her, "What is a trilogy, Mom?" Though he had not understood the term, he had been most impressed by the Tolkien tales. Clearly, if books move children this deeply, parents need not worry that they are being comprehended.

Don't worry if your child constantly seeks out easy books, far below his instructional reading level. There may be many

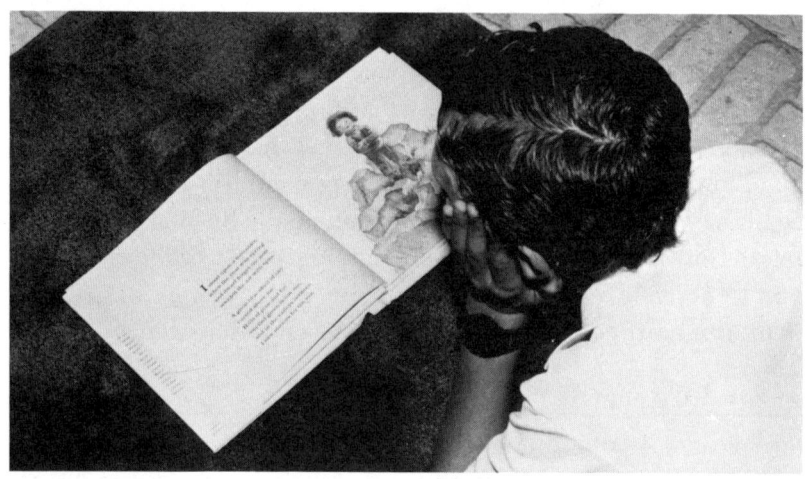

Just like adults, children sometimes choose books far below their reading level, simply for fun.

reasons for this type of behavior, and it is not something to be anxious about. If a child is being pushed into reading materials that are difficult at school, he or she will want to be certain that reading is fun when it's for relaxation. Your child may become "stuck" on certain types of books, such as those on the easy-to-read shelf at the library, and read only those books for quite a long while. You yourself may remember reading every book in the *Nancy Drew* or the *Hardy Boys* series. These kinds of books sometimes dominate the reading material of children for as long as a year at a time. If you refrain from criticizing your child's reading material and present him or her with alternatives, the child will soon grow out of this phase.

If your child is reading from a narrow range of literature or is reading very easy books, it is even more important to read aloud from different types of materials. Select some books at the library other than those the child is selecting, so that your child has access to lots of different kinds of books.

Choosing books to share with children gives them access to literature they might not select for themselves.

Don't be concerned if your child selects "inferior" books. Parents sometimes react by pushing "good" books or well-known books upon their children. It is helpful to remember that unless children read "poor" books (with shallow plots or unimaginative characters) they will never learn to discriminate the "good" from the "bad," the boring from the exciting, or the original from the trite. Further, you must be certain that your child has many opportunities to select books on his own. Only when they are able to find pleasurable reading material on their own will children view reading as recreation.

Chapter 4

Word Recognition

Child: "Let's have a banquet (pronounced ban kay)."
Dad: "A what?"
Child: "A banquet (ban kay). You know, like *ballet* and *chalet*. It means a feast!"

Reading is the intricate combination of a variety of strategies for processing printed language until meaning is clear. Your child needs to be able to use a variety of strategies to recognize the words that are on the printed page.

It is important for children to recognize that, unless they understand what they are attempting to read, they are not really reading. If we focus attention on skills in isolation instead of reading real stories, we contribute to teaching the child that merely recognizing and pronouncing words is reading. The best way to help your child learn word-recognition strategies is by encouraging reading and by reading to the child. After repeated exposure to words in stories, he or she learns to use context to figure out what a word means. He or she learns that words have parts that provide clues to meanings (structural analysis); that some words have distinctive shapes (configuration); and that some sound patterns are consistent (phonics). But by far the most important thing the reader learns is *when* it is appropriate to use each strategy.

Reading is not an accumulation of basic skills that, when mastered, permit a child to get meaning from a page. Rather, reading is a holistic process that uses a number of strategies to unlock meaning from unfamiliar content. Most children memorize stories and gradually match print to the words they already know from their memorized reading. Thus, most children learn their first words in context. They recognize story characters' names and can find them on each page of the book. Gradually, children's guesses become sight words, identified in any context. If you wrote the word on a list, the child would recognize it. In conjunction with identifying words in context come the other word-analysis strategies that are presented in this chapter: sight words, key words, structural analysis, configuration, and phonics.

Context

Using context is how we adults usually piece together the meaning of unknown words. We skip the word we don't know and see if the passage makes sense without it. In the same way, your child needs to practice guessing what words mean from the story he or she is reading.

It is hard for your child to think of two things at once—how words are pronounced and what a passage means. Poor readers pay attention to "getting the words right" while good readers focus on "understanding the message."

Using context, if a passage does not make sense, your child will stop, go back, and make sense out of it before proceeding. Good readers self-correct all the time. Poor readers keep right on going, even if what they are reading makes no sense at all. The context reader does not notice incorrect pronunciation. So, your child might read, "The man lived in an enormous *museum* (instead of *mansion*)," pause, and go back to correct the mistake. But he would read right on when pronouncing "banquet" as ban-kay, "conspiracy" as con-spire-a-cy, or "Thomas" with a "th" sound. When your child begins to depend upon context clues, he will read faster and with more expression.

How can you help your child develop context skills? Read from books that have unknown words in them (and most books have at least several). *Caps for Sale,* by Esphyr Slobodkina, begins, "Once there was a peddler who sold caps." The word *peddler* needs no explanation. It is obvious from the story that the peddler moves around selling caps. At the beginning reader level, it is important not to stick with specially written, vocabulary-controlled reading materials. Controlled-vocabulary materials are less predictable for beginning readers because the language does not match their own language, thus making reading more difficult. If children only encounter controlled vocabulary in their books, they have fewer chances to develop their reading context skills.

When your child is beginning to read and comes to an unfamiliar word or makes a mistake, resist the temptation to provide the word or correct the reading. Wait until the child has finished the sentence; then, if the child doesn't go back and correct the error, ask, "Does that make sense? Want to try it again?" If *you* provide the word, you are depriving your child of opportunities to use context to uncover meaning. Also, don't ask the beginning reader to "sound it out" when he encounters a new word. This, too, would deny him the opportunity to use context.

Since your child continues to learn how to use context after being able to read, it is important to keep reading aloud even after he or she has learned to read. By listening to stories that are more difficult than the ones he or she can read independently, the child is gaining sophistication in using context to derive meaning from unfamiliar words. The more children can encounter unfamiliar words (in songs and fingerplays, for example) the more practice they will have at using context skills. Even the sometimes archaic language of Mother Goose is helpful in this regard.

Sight Words

In order to be a fluent reader, your child needs to recognize a large number of words by sight. If the child has to stop and analyze each word, he or she will be a very slow reader. Slow readers are rarely avid readers. Early methods of teaching reading used to emphasize having a child memorize by sight lists of words that were then included in simple stories in basals. Maybe you can remember the "Dick and Jane and Spot" readers. In these, children memorized the words *Dick, Jane, Spot, run, to,* etc., and then were able to read passages like "Run, Spot, run. Run to Dick. Run. Run. Run!" Of course, these stories were devoid of any real meaning, so they overemphasized sight strategies at the expense of context.

There are several ways you can help your child learn sight

Matching familiar words is the first step in helping a child learn words by sight.

words. A first step is being able to match familiar words. For example, make word cards and see if your child can match each card to the right word in a book. Pick words that are names at first.

While reading *Curious George,* by H.A. Rey, you might suggest, "This is the word *George.* Can you find another place where it says *George* on this page?" From recognizing the word in the book, your child can move to learning to recognize the word in other contexts.

Once they learn to read a character's name, children soon recognize that name in other contexts.

Your child may want you to make a list of the words he or she can recognize by sight. If you start a list of familiar words from stories or the names of friends or foods, he or she may request new words. It is harder to read a word on a list than it is in context.

Another method that may help your child acquire a sight vocabulary is to write for him or her. You'll use words over and over again when you write, causing your child to recognize them.

Key Words

Sylvia Ashton Warner, a teacher from New Zealand, has written a book called *Teacher* (Simon & Schuster, 1971) which details her approach to teaching reading. She asks a child what word he would like to learn each day. On a big card, with the child watching, she writes the word, reciting each letter as it is formed. The child then traces over the letters with a finger, copies the word, and reads the word over and over again.

These words become the child's "key words." Favorite key words are likely to be the names of friends and family members, words for foods, activities, animals, and colorful verbs. One parent made a word box for his daughter's key words. Annie eagerly volunteered to read her words for any visitor. By collecting the words your child can read by sight, you can soon write little messages for your child using mainly those words, and your child will be astounded that he or she can actually read. You need to be careful not to push your child into learning key

A child may enjoy keeping a collection of favorite words he can read by sight.

Growing Up Reading

words. Ashton-Warner recommends throwing away any words that your child does not remember by the next day. Those words, she claims, are not really key words or they would have been remembered. She cautions not to drill children on words they don't remember, for sessions will rapidly deteriorate if you focus on the words your child does not know. Instead, collect the words your child *can* read and build upon those successes. If your child is older, he or she might enjoy collecting unusual vocabulary words. A collection called *365 New Words for Kids Calendar*, available from the Workman Publishing Company, 1 West 39th Street, New York, NY 10018, is a clever way to systematically study new words.

Structural Analysis

Structural analysis helps us to divide words into their parts—root words and affixes (prefixes or suffixes). If, for example, your child came to the word *untied*, he or she might recognize by sight the root word *tie*, and the prefix *un*, which means not, and be able to put the meaning together, as *not tied*. Structural analysis can help your child understand what words mean.

Prefixes and Suffixes
Once you get started exploring word origins with your child, you'll get hooked on words.

One parent found the Latin word *jectus*, meaning throw, which in English becomes the root *ject*. She and her daughter generated a list of *ject* words:
1. reject — *re* is back and *ject* is throw, so throw back is the meaning of reject. Reject that lie! or Reject that fish—throw it back!
2. project — *pro* means forward; *ject* means throw. Project means to throw forward. Scientists can project missiles into space.
3. interject — *inter* means between; *ject* means to throw. Interject means to throw or insert between. To interject a comment would be to throw it or insert it between someone else's comments.

One could go on and on discovering the relationships between the root words and their affixes. Games can be made where roots are matched to their affixes.

Some of the most frequently recurring prefixes and their meanings are in the following chart.

Common Prefixes

Prefix	Meaning	Example
dis-	not; opposite of	disappear, disobey, disagree, distrust
com-; con-; col-	with; together; at the same time	combine, concur, collide, connect
in-; im-; il-; ir-	not	illegal, incorrect, irresponsible, imperfect
mis-	bad; badly; wrongly	mistake, misbehave, misunderstand, misfire
pre-	before	prefix, predawn, preschool, prehistoric
anti-	against	antitoxin, antitrust, antifreeze, antisocial
super-	over; above; superior to	superman, supermarket, supernatural, superpower
non-	not	nonalcoholic, nonsense, nonskid, nonprofit
tri-	three	triangle, tricolor, trinity, tricycle
em-; en-	in; into	embrace, employ, enlist, endanger
de-	reversal; opposite of; from	decrease, decontrol, dehydrate, defrost
inter-	between; among	interact, interfere, interweave, intermingle
ex-	out of; away from	excavate, expel, exhale, exit

Prefix	Meaning	Examples
sub-	under; beneath	subway, submarine, subfreezing, subhead
auto-	directed from within; self; same	automatic, automobile, autograph, autobiography
bi-	two	bicycle, biannual, bilingual, bisect
mid-	middle	midnight, midday, midterm, Midwest
re-	again; back; backwards	react, rebuild, recopy, recycle, retreat, recoil
un-	not; opposite of	unable, unbroken, unpolished, unsalted

You would not want to drill your child on the meanings of these prefixes, but they might be used as the basis for dictionary games—which of several prefixes appears in more words? How many words do you recognize using a particular prefix? Making lists of words using a prefix is a good car game or rainy day activity.

Common Suffixes

Suffix	Function	Examples
-tion	changes a verb into a noun	suggestion, reaction, subtraction
-er	makes an adjective comparison	taller, finer, happier
-er; -or; -ar	means one who does something	officer, author, scholar, surveyor
-ant; -ent	changes a verb into an adjective	reliant, defiant, subservient
-ness	changes an adjective into a noun	happiness, sadness, meekness

-ity	changes an adjective into a noun	security, nicety activity
-y	changes a noun into an adjective	sunny, curly, bubbly
-able	changes a verb into an adjective	teachable, enjoyable, readable
-less	changes a noun into an adjective	helpless, moneyless, careless
-ful	changes a noun into an adjective	helpful, merciful, playful
-ist	one who practices	typist, cyclist, violinist

There are many other suffixes that occur less frequently. Both prefixes and suffixes appear often enough that your child will learn them as he or she reads. Informal, oral word-play and games, however, can sensitize a child to the parts of words so that he or she is more likely to take notice of word parts when reading.

Compound Words

When your child can recognize compound words, he or she is able to guess their meanings easily. Instead of thinking of the word *timetable* in little parts (ti me ta ble), if the child can recognize *time* and *table,* he or she will come up with the meaning of the word more quickly. You and your child might enjoy figuring out the meanings of words such as:

armchair	cupboard	grandma	grapefruit	streetcar
baseball	doghouse	thanksgiving	understand	tablespoon
bedspread	farmhouse	seaweed	horseshoe	toothbrush
bookcase	foghorn	mousetrap	overcoat	tablecloth
bullfrog	headlight	pancake	classroom	wishbone

You might try coining your own compound words by combining two smaller words in a way that makes sense. You don't want your child to memorize compound words and their meanings, but together you can informally learn them by reading and by playing word games with the family.

Words are constantly being invented and changed in meaning. Does your child have a hobby or a special interest? Every hobby has its own collection of specialized vocabulary. There is a vocabulary for cooking, sewing, athletics, and almost every area of human endeavor. Musical vocabularies consist of Italian terms, while ballet vocabularies are mainly French in origin.

Structural analysis, then, can help your child recognize words he or she cannot recognize by sight or figure out through context. Structural analysis helps children avoid becoming slow readers and helps them continue to focus on the meaning of a word rather than its sound.

Configuration

Several games which are popular with children help them focus on the configurations of words. Games in which you build words by guessing individual letters force players to focus on the way the word looks. Find-a-word puzzles contain words written in all directions. Children must find words hidden in a maze of letters.

THE FAMILY CIRCUS. **By Bil Keane**

"No, that isn't a word either."

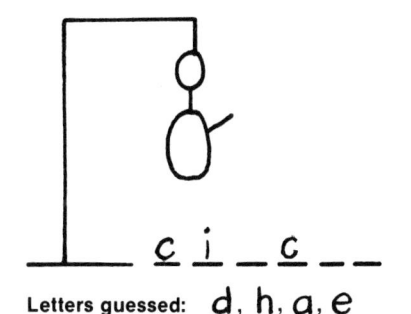

In "Hangman" children try to guess the letters that make up a word before they have a whole "man" to hang. Each time they make an incorrect guess, another body part is added.

Letters guessed: d, h, a, e

By informally playing word games, children acquire sensitivity to the way words look. That is as far as you need to go in "teaching" this word-analysis strategy.

Phonics

Do you ever tell your child to "sound out" a word? Sounding out is using the word-analysis skill called phonics. You can't sound out all words, but when context and structural analysis fail, it is helpful for a child to be able to sound out words. But sounding out should be a last resort for word analysis because children who depend on phonics are slow readers. They don't concentrate as much on getting meaning from what they are reading.

Long words can be divided into syllables using these rules:
- all syllables have a vowel sound.
- a final *e* in a syllable does not add another sound or syllable (cake, lake, spike).
- when there are two consonants between two vowels, the syllables are divided between the two consonants (pen cil; bal let).
- when there is a consonant between two vowels, the syllable is divided after the first vowel (be gin; ba na na).
- when *-le* is preceded by a consonant, the division is made before the consonant (han dle; la dle).

There are other rules, but they don't work as regularly as these do.

As a reading skill, syllables help your child see words in parts, rather than having to look at each alphabet letter separately. Fluent readers see whole groups of words at one time. Beginning readers usually stop and look at each word (or syllable or letter) when they encounter a new story. They need strategies for moving away from looking at individual letters. The larger the unit that your child can comprehend, the faster he or she can read and the more he or she can focus on the meaning of the passage.

Has your child noticed beginning sounds like *T*, for Timmy, Tommy, Terry, and Tanya? Almost all of the consonants have just one representative sound. Exceptions include the letters *g* and *c*, which can be hard (usually if they precede the letters *a*, *o*, or *u*—*cake, gate, coat, goat, guard,* and *cute*) or soft (usually if they precede the letters *e* or *i*—*gent, cent, gentle, city,* and *ginger*). *Q* is always followed by a *u* and makes the *kw* sound. *S* is sometimes *s* as in *less*, sometimes *z* as in *nose*, and sometimes *sh* as in *sure*.

When your child comes to an unfamiliar word, he or she will identify it a lot faster if he or she can use both context and initial consonants as clues. There are lots of fun ways to help your child learn initial consonants.

A common activity is to cut pictures out of magazines and make alphabet books, collages, or other collections of words that

While making word collections, children learn that initial sounds are good clues to pronouncing words.

begin with the same sounds. When making such word collections, you will want to label each item so that your child can see that initial letters are usually a good indicator of how the word sounds. It will also be obvious that some sounds have several spellings. Right from the beginning, children can learn that *k* represents the *k* sound, as does *c* in some instances.

After your child has learned initial consonant sounds, he'll probably skip to end, or final, consonant sounds. Vowels are really not necessary for decoding new words. You can probably read words without vowels in them: *m-th-r, h-rs-, -ppl-,* and *gl-ss-s* are recognizable as *mother, horse, apple,* and *glasses.* Therefore, it is natural that children seem to learn consonants before vowels.

After your child has mastered single consonants, he'll pick up consonant blends where two or more consonants appear together. The following chart shows words with common blends:

Initial Blends

blend	frown	scrap	spill	school
brown	glue	skate	stop	scratch
clean	green	slip	swim	split
crown	play	smell	train	spring
fly	prance	snap	twins	street

Final Blends

first	want	lift	felt	harp
mask	spend	milk	help	
wasp	camp	skunk	mold	

Sometimes, when two consonants or vowels appear together, they make one sound and are called digraphs:

Beginning Digraphs

| churn | this | sharp | when |
| thanks | those | phone | |

Ending Digraphs

| lurch | wash | myth | graph |

After learning consonant sounds in words, your child probably will pay more attention to vowel sounds, which are far

---

Growing Up Reading

more complex. Vowels can have a long sound (*lake, seat, fight, soap,* and *use*) or a short sound (*hat, pet, hit, hot, hut*) or several other sounds. There are many rules that govern the use of vowels.

There are literally hundreds of phonics rules. Most of them are fraught with exceptions and those that are not are used so seldom as to be almost useless.

Opportunities to use phonics occur regularly in children's books. Some authors write rhyming stories with patterned words repeated. Dr. Seuss, in *One Fish, Two Fish, Red Fish, Blue Fish,* and P.D. Eastman, in *Go, Dog, Go,* give children practice using phonics. Some books have non-word sounds as a part of the text. In *Roar And More* by Karla Kuskin, the dog goes "arf," "woof," and "bark," the bee goes "bzzzspzz" across a page, and so forth. These written sound words have to be read phonetically.

Since phonics slows a child down while he or she thinks about the individual parts of words, your child would not want to rely solely on phonics to identify a word. If the child is having difficulty reading a new word, encourage him or her to guess what it might be. What would make sense at that point?

Frequently, a good strategy in reading is to skip a word. Sometimes meaning can only emerge in what comes after—*even if* the child was able to sound it out—e.g., "The girl had tears in her [dress, eyes]." The pronunciation *and* meaning are determined by the rest of the sentence.

Chapter 5

Reading Is Everywhere

"Everywhere there is reading. There is reading about Smokey the Bear on the bus. There is reading on the Nutty O's box. Everywhere there is reading or writing, writing or reading."
Quote from Jim in *When Will I Read?* by Miriam Cohen. (Illustrated by Lillian Hoban.) New York: Greenwillow, 1977.

Have you ever looked for opportunities to read with your child other than reading aloud? Our children grow up in a print-oriented society. For example, I once counted fifty billboards and signs on a half-mile stretch of highway. Captions and advertising on television expose children to writing. At the grocery store children see hundreds of signs and labels. It is no wonder that children can learn to read so easily.

With innumerable opportunities for reading in the environment, you can consciously plan to make use of them. It is much quicker and easier to cook or shop without your child, yet including your child in these errands provides many opportunities for informal reading experiences as well as developing a sense of togetherness. When your child sees reading in numerous different settings, he or she learns the importance of learning to read. Such experiences are a terrific motivation for learning to read.

In this chapter there are many ideas for integrating reading into your daily routines while cooking, shopping, traveling, singing, reading music, and following directions. I hope these ideas will serve as springboards, stimulating you to think of many other techniques that will expose your child to reading and develop his or her critical reasoning skills.

Cooking

Children of all ages love to cook. It makes them feel grown up to be able to help adults prepare foods. Older children enjoy the independence which accompanies cooking activities. In this day and age, both boys and girls need to learn how to cook so that they can take care of themselves or contribute equally to the maintenance of a household.

There are many reasons why you might want to share cooking activities with your children. They are more likely to eat what they have helped prepare. Cooking also provides a happy time for you and your child to exchange ideas. While waiting for the water to boil, you have an opportunity to talk, which would not occur if the child were watching television while you prepared the meal. It is all too tempting to let the television babysit. Single parents especially might find meal preparation a difficult time in the evenings when there is no other adult to play with the children while the evening meal is being prepared.

Sharing cooking activities provides a time for togetherness and for practicing reading skills as well.

Letting your child help you cook the meal can bring you together and make the task more enjoyable as well.

It is not easier to cook with your child, but it can be more fun. First, you have to recognize that there will be spills and mistakes. Even you spill once in a while. When a spill occurs, it is important not to scold your child, who already feels bad about the accident. Rather, say, "Let's clean it up," and give him or her a rag to join you in the cleanup.

Here's how cooking can help your child in reading:
- It shows a useful reason for learning to read.
- It exposes your child to reading abbreviations that are seldom seen in other books. (oz., lb., T., tsp.)
- It gives experience with numerals and fractions, which are not frequently seen in most books.
- It encourages precise reading of details as opposed to the more rapid reading of books.
- It demands reading in sequence.
- It provides rereading experience (practice) as you check out whether each step has been completed.
- It logically ties in with other reading experiences (slogans, brand names, reading packages) and writing experiences (shopping lists and recipes to share with others).

With all of these unique benefits, cooking is an activity you don't want to overlook!

When you first cook with your child, read the directions or the recipes, pointing to the words so that your child can see where the information is coming from. Your older children can read and follow the directions by themselves.

For parents who are hesitant about having very young children use the stove or sharp utensils, there is a cookbook with simple recipes that require neither. It is called *Pickle in the Middle and Other Easy Snacks*, by Frances Zeifel (Harper & Row, 1979). Another recipe book recommended for very young children is *Pease Porridge Hot: A Mother Goose Cookbook*, by Lorinda Bryan Cauley (G.P. Putnam's Sons, 1977). Cookbook reading can provide your child with practice at high levels of reasoning. One parent bought a flip-card recipe book which her child read avidly, selecting recipes that looked good. This led to writing shopping lists and preparing a special family meal once a week.

There are two basic kinds of cooking that you'll want to do with your children. One is to make special things—snacks, desserts, and sweets for special occasions or holidays. The other is regular meal preparation. The latter is far more important because it fits into routines. Just as with any skill, the more you practice it, the better you become at doing it.

There are a number of cookbooks especially written for children. Several are listed here.

Huang, Paul C. *The Illustrated Step-by-Step Beginner's Cookbook.* Illustrated by Joseph Daniel Fiedler and Michael McQuaide. New York: Four Winds Press, 1980.

Katzman, Susan Manlin. *For Kids Who Cook: Recipes and Treats.* Illustrated by Edward J. Kohorst. New York: Holt, Rinehart and Winston, 1977.

Steinkoler, Ronnie. *A Jewish Cookbook for Children.* Illustrated by Sonja Glassman. New York: Julian Messner, 1980.

Watson, Pauline, and editors of Cricket Magazine. *Cricket's Cookery.* Illustrated by Marlin Hafner. New York: Random House, 1977.

Your child might want to begin his own favorite recipe collections in either a recipe file or a recipe book format. With his own cookbook, he can share recipes with other children. Some neighborhoods have developed a neighborhood recipe collection by sharing recipes at parties and holiday gatherings. You might try having a recipe party, where each child attending brings a favorite snack along with copies of the recipe for everyone in attendance.

Several other party ideas come from children's books. In *The Best-Loved Doll* by Rebecca Caudill (Holt, Rinehart, and Winston, 1962), each character brings a favorite doll to a party. Similarly, the child in *May I Bring A Friend?* by Beatrice de Regniers (Atheneum, 1964) shows up at a tea party with a different animal friend each time. Your child might enjoy having tea parties for his or her stuffed animals or dolls. He or she can prepare the snacks for parties and write invitations as well. A child who wants a surprise party for his birthday really gets one in *The Surprise Party* by Annabelle Prager (Pantheon, 1977).

Picnic foods are easy to prepare and fun to eat. Books about

Party ideas in books prompt children to plan social gatherings of their own.

picnics include *Once We Went on a Picnic* by Aileen Fisher (Thomas Y. Crowell, 1975) and *My Kitchen* by Harlow Rockwell (Greenwillow, 1980). In the latter, a boy tells how his lunch is made.

There are quite a few nonfiction books about foods. Examples include:

Williams, Vera B. *It's a Gingerbread House: Bake It, Build It, Eat It!* New York: Greenwillow Books, 1978.

Woodside, Dave. *What Makes Popcorn Pop?* Illustrated by Kay Woon. New York: Atheneum, 1980.

Many, many children's books either contain cooking activities or refer to foods in such a way that cooking would be an ideal way to extend the book with a follow-up cooking activity. Some of these are traditional tales, others are fiction stories (many of them humorous), and others are related to holidays. Several are poetry or song collections. Here are some recommended books which might inspire cooking activities:

Barrett, Judi. *Cloudy with a Chance of Meatballs.* Illustrated by Ron Barrett. New York: Atheneum, 1978.

Brown, Marcia. *Stone Soup.* New York: Charles Scribner's Sons, 1947.

Carle, Eric, *Pancakes, Pancakes.* New York: Alfred. A. Knopf, 1970.
——. *The Very Hungry Caterpillar.* New York: Philomel Books, 1969.
De Paola, Tomie. *Pancakes for Breakfast.* New York: Harcourt Brace Jovanovich, 1978.
Galdone, Paul. *The Gingerbread Boy.* Boston: Houghton Mifflin, 1975.
Hurwitz, Johanna. *Aldo Applesauce.* Illustrated by John Wallner. New York: William R. Morrow, 1979.
Marshall, James. *Yummers.* Boston: Houghton Mifflin, 1973.
McCloskey, Robert. *Blueberries for Sal.* New York: Viking, 1948.
Patz, Nancy. *Pumpernickel Tickle and Mean Green Cheese.* New York: Franklin Watts, 1978.
Sendak, Maurice. *Chicken Soup with Rice.* New York: Harper & Row, 1962.
Seuss, Dr. *Green Eggs and Ham.* New York: Random House, 1960.

As all of these books touching on foods and cooking indicate, the link between cooking and reading is a very strong one.

Shopping

It's ten o'clock Saturday morning and you are at the grocery store. Your oldest child just dropped the cookie the bakery lady gave him and the youngest is systematically pulling cans from the shelf. You wonder if it is worth it to bring the kids with you. Like cooking, shopping can be a family routine with an infinite number of opportunities for reading experiences, both for preschoolers and for much older children who can refine their critical-reading skills by analyzing product names and labels. As with cooking, it may be far more convenient to go shopping without your children. It is faster and you don't have to deal with their requests for products you don't want or need. Omitting your children from shopping outings, however, not only deprives them of opportunities for reading but also limits their growing economic sense and mathematical reasoning.

Do you make a shopping list each week? If so, you might consider letting your child help. Then, when you are shopping, he or she can read the list and cross items off as they are gathered into the grocery cart.

Helping with the shopping list offers additional reading opportunities for a child.

How about redeeming coupons? One family I know allows the children to keep the proceeds from any coupon they collect and redeem at the store while shopping. The family decides if the item is really needed and a good value, and if it is, they redeem the coupon.

On your shopping trip there are many reading opportunities. You might help your child classify the foods on the list into sections at the store: dairy, meat, canned goods, bakery, deli, fruits and vegetables, or household supplies. One grocery store, after being renovated, published a map for its customers to follow in finding the new locations of products. Do you take advantage of sales? Let your child help! He or she can read labels and prices to determine the best values for the products on your list.

Food labels could provide an entire reading curriculum. A fascinating book for children is *What's in a Name: Famous Brand Names*, by Arnold Oren Read (Julian Messner, 1979). It's fascinating to study the persuasive use of language through an examination of product names and labels.

Your child can help determine values by comparing the quality and prices of different products.

Names used in conjunction with products include Uncle Ben, Aunt Jemina, Hungry Jack, Mr. Muscle, Mr. Clean, and the Jolly Green Giant. Uncles and aunts are relatives with most pleasant connotations. The items with the Hungry Jack label must be satisfying. Mr. Muscle and Mr. Clean obviously do hard cleaning tasks. And the Jolly Green Giant grows better vegetables because they are large. Moreover, he is a jolly gardener!

Fabric softeners all have soft-sounding names: Final Touch, Nu-Soft, Rain Barrel (Is rain water really softer?), Lemon Fluff, and Downy (softer than a feather).

One could go on and on with different analyses of product labels and advertising slogans. Suffice it to say that the study of labels makes your child more aware of words and enhances his or her vocabulary. It shows the multiple uses of words, their subtle meanings, and the power words have to convey feelings and impressions. Your child learns to recognize propaganda techniques in other reading contexts also, by reading for details and with precision. By reading package sizes and weights and by comparing prices for products, he or she learns to read abbreviations and numerals that don't often appear in books.

Your child analyzes and draws conclusions about his or her findings, two very sophisticated reading and thinking skills.

Shopping, then, can give you and your family lots of interesting reading experiences. A children's book called *The Supermarket*, by Anne and Harlow Rockwell (Macmillan, 1979), might stimulate more ideas. Including children on our shopping adventures gives them a weekly informal reading lesson in addition to helping them become wise consumers.

Traveling

Trips abound in opportunities for reading and writing. Like cooking and shopping, taking a trip with your child can be either a tedious, tiring experience or a challenging and rewarding one. Even on short trips, your child will have time on his or her hands. However, children can use these moments both to learn and to entertain themselves.

You might want to store books in the car in a special book box. That way every time your child enters the car, there is something for him or her to do, and the child develops the habit of looking for it. There are many children's activity books available in drugstores and bookstores. Though some of these amount to little more than coloring books, many include crossword puzzles, find-a-word games, and thinking games.

Before you start a trip, your child can help plan the route you'll take and any stops you might make.

Growing Up Reading

In addition, there are many reading opportunities outside of the car. Can your child read street signs, traffic signs, and route numbers? Does he or she notice advertising and storefront signs?

You can put some variety into daily commuting trips by making a homemade map for your child to follow as you drive along. This initial experience helps him or her interpret regular road maps. One parent had a road atlas in the car. He taught his daughter how to use the key to find places on the maps. After that, she spent many hours locating places while she was commuting to and from school.

Longer trips provide even more reading activities. When your child is actively involved in the planning he or she tends to be more enthusiastic. Well before the start of the trip, you might help your child write away for advertising materials about the places you are going to visit. Chambers of Commerce almost always deliver a courteous response. National parks, recreation areas, historical houses, and state tourist departments are other good sources of information. When traveling, virtually every state has a "welcome" area where maps and tourist information are distributed. Your route can be plotted on a map so that your child can follow as you go along. Following the route on a map eliminates many annoying questions about when the next stop will come and how much farther it is to your destination.

Prior to leaving on a trip, find some books about the places you plan to visit. Check through the subject guide in your local library to find books about places on your trip. The American Library Association publishes annotated bibliographies of children's books grouped by region of the country. Fiction books whose settings are in the region are listed in addition to nonfiction books. These books may be about specific places, or a collection of information on a topic, such as:

Van Steenwyck, Elizabeth. *Presidents at Home.* New York: Julian Messner, 1980. Contains not only information about all of the presidents' homes but also directions for finding them.

Ronan, Margaret. *All about Our 50 States.* Illustrated by William Meyerriecks. New York: Random House, 1978. Anthology of useful information for young travelers.

There are books written about practically all of our

National Parks. An example is *Mammoth Cave National Park* by Ruth Radlauer. Photos by Ed Radlauer. Chicago: Children's Press, 1978.

Have you ever visited a local public library when you've been on a trip? That's an excellent way to find books about the places you are visiting. Local public libraries usually have a section for local interest materials. You'll discover many interesting things about the places you visit and see things that you'd otherwise have missed. Information about local personalities, often found at public libraries, can bring an added dimension to your visit.

The way you travel can be a source of fascination for your young traveler. *Charlie Brown's Third Super Book of Questions and Answers: About All Kinds of Boats and Planes, Cars and Trains and Other Things That Move!* (Random House, 1978) will provide hours of attentive concentration. If your family is traveling by air, there is *Superplanes* by John Gabriel Navarra (Doubleday, 1979).

If your child is curious about other types of vehicles, he or she might enjoy:

Marston, Hope Irvin. *Big Rigs.* New York: Dodd, Mead, 1979.
Radlauer, Ed. *Some Basics About Vans.* Chicago: Children's Press, 1978.
Richards, Norman, and Pat Richards. *Trucks and Supertrucks.* New York: Doubleday, 1980.

Have you ever tried to spot license plates from each state of

Looking for license plates from each state helps pass the time and gives practice in reading while traveling.

Growing Up Reading

the Union as you drove a long distance? Bring a blank map of the United States to help chart the states of license plates that your family sees. While waiting in a long line of cars and trucks en route to a ferry ride, one child recorded many states and provincial license plates. Her quest made the hour's wait in the hot sunshine pass quickly.

Along the road there are billboards, which provide another interesting language lesson. Your family can collect and analyze advertising techniques used on billboards. Your child might also enjoy keeping track of mileage markers, road signs, and exit numbers.

Your family has probably invented many other car games. Try an alphabet game. Each person in turn thinks of a word beginning with the succeeding letter of the alphabet. You can make the game more complex by limiting the category in which words must fall (foods, fruits, things that move, animals). The same game, where each person alternately calls out things, can be played with colors (list as many things as you can that are green) or with sizes (each person thinking of something slightly larger than the previously mentioned item).

Have you ever wondered how cities and streets got their names? There are several cities and villages in this country with the same name. Street names are even more repetitious. And the origins of both are fascinating.

Children's stories come alive when you visit the places where they were written. Whole tourist centers have developed from the sites of several famous children's stories. Literally millions of children have visited the island of Chincoteague, site of the adventures of *Misty, Sea Star,* and *Stormy, Misty's Foal* by Marguerite Henry. On "Pony Penning Day," thousands stand on the shore to watch the wild ponies swim the channel. The sites of Laura Ingalls Wilder's homes have become popular tourist spots. The village of Chittenango, New York, where L. Frank Baum was born, has paved its sidewalks with yellow brick, a symbol of the yellow brick road in his Oz stories. The home of Marjorie Kinnard Rawlings, author of *The Yearling,* is a county museum in Cross Creek, Florida.

Provide your child with biographies when visiting New Salem, Monticello, Mount Vernon, and other famous sites.

The settings of some children's stories are as important as are the characters. A visit to Nantucket Island would be incomplete without sharing the *Obadiah* books, by Brinton Turkle, about a Quaker family who lived on the island in the nineteenth century. Similarly, many of Robert McCloskey's books are set in New England—along the coast of Maine or on the Boston Common. If you share these books with your child while visiting the places, the books come alive. Examples of some recent books on historical topics whose settings might be visited include:

Hall, Donald. *The Ox-Cart Man.* Illustrated by Barbara Cooney. New York: Viking, 1979 (Portsmouth Harbor).

Provensen, Alice and Martin. *The Glorious Flight across the English Channel.* New York: Random House, 1974.

Smucker, Barbara. *Runaway to Freedom.* Illustrated by Charles Lilly. New York: Harper and Row, 1978.

There are many more. Read stories about wars and battles prior to visiting battlefields and stories about people of different cultures before visiting other countries or cultural groups in this country.

If your family enjoys camping, you'll notice that most campgrounds provide maps of their campgrounds which help orient visitors. Reading books before bed by lantern light is an especially treasured camping experience. Our family will long remember reading Joan Aiken's *The Wolves of Willoughby Chase* by flashlight in our tent at a campground.

Travel, then, can either be the tedious experience of dragging the children along, or it can be an educational pot of gold. Reading makes traveling more interesting and more fun.

Music

Remember how singing used to soothe your baby when he or she was fussing? Have you noticed how songs and finger games captivate preschoolers? One of the best ways to prepare for reading is by singing. If your child has learned to read the words in songs, it will expand his or her vocabulary and increase comprehension.

Your family might enjoy a good children's songbook. Here are some:

Bierhorst, John. *A Cry from the Earth: Music of the North American Indians.* New York: Four Winds Press, 1979.

Dallin, Leon and Lynn. *Heritage Songster: 334 Folk and Familiar Songs.* 2nd ed. Dubuque, Ia.: William C. Brown Company, 1980.

Glazer, Tom. *Eye Winker, Tom Tinker, Chin Chopper: Fifty Musical Fingerplays.* New York: Doubleday, 1973.

———. *Do Your Ears Hang Low? Fifty More Musical Fingerplays.* Illustrated by Mila Lazarevich. New York: Doubleday, 1980.

John, Timothy, and Peter Hankey, editors. *The Great Song Book.* Illustrated by Tomi Ungerer. New York: Doubleday, 1978.

Langstaff, John, compiler. *Hot Cross Buns and Other Old Street Cries.* Illustrated by Nancy Winslow Parker. New York: Atheneum, 1978.

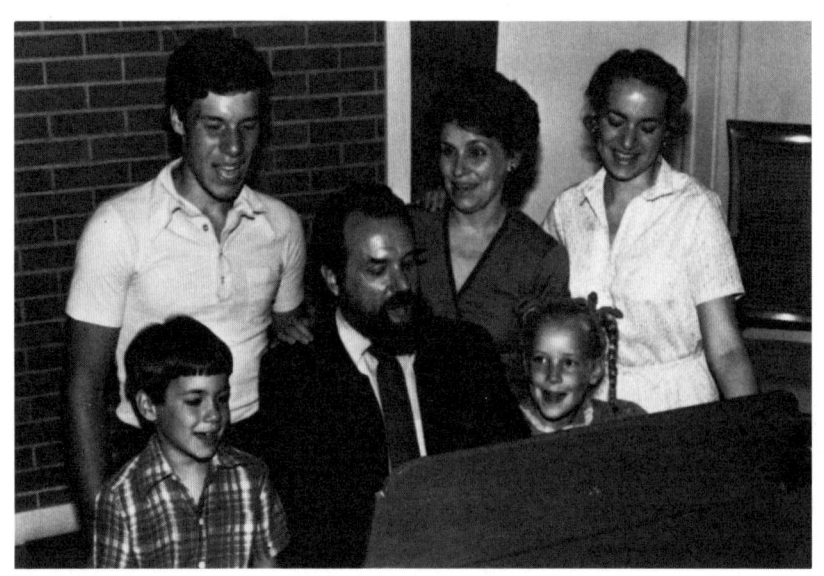

Singing together prepares young children for reading, expands vocabulary and comprehension, and provides delightful family entertainment.

Your family might enjoy singing together for half an hour each evening. Collection books are also fun to take on a trip in the car, or you can make your own songbook. Write the words to favorite songs in a spiral-bound notebook. Before long, your preschooler can actually read the songs because he or she already knows what the words are. You can also write the words of favorite songs on looseleaf paper, cover the pages with clear plastic, and place them in a looseleaf binder to make your own favorite songbook collection.

If your child reads hymnals at church or Sunday School, he or she has learned how to read verses, skipping from one line of print to the next and then returning for later verses. One two-year-old, whose parents had sung hymns to her since she was a baby, could find her favorite hymn in the hymnal long before she could read.

If your family gathers together at holiday times, you can sing songs. In some neighborhoods, caroling is a tradition at Christmas. Children who have memorized some of the carols have an easy time reading the music. Your older child might enjoy researching the origins of the lyrics and the tunes and comparing the many different versions of carols. Some carols are easy to learn to sing in a foreign language.

Reading music is not difficult because children are fascinated with codes. The musical code is a rather easy one to break. There are essentially two elements to it. One is pitch. The notes either go up or down. The distance between the notes represents the distance between the pitches that are sung. The other is tempo. Once you learn the few mathematical relationships between whole notes, half notes, quarter notes, and eighth notes, you can read music! It is easier to learn to read the music of familiar songs at first. Sight reading new songs can come later.

Music can also help your child's reading comprehension. Many songs tell stories with interesting word usage. The vocabulary and expressions in songs are a study in themselves. What do the lyrics mean? Your child might enjoy making up new lyrics to familiar old tunes. Songs have interesting histories. There are a number of biographies of famous composers that are written for children.

Some songs have been made into picture books. These are extremely popular with children of all ages. They usually have the music on the last page along with a bit of history about the song. Good song picture books have the lyrics spaced so that one stanza is on a page, for easy page turning after each phrase. Since you want your child to read by phrase (not by letter or by word), reading song picture books helps focus on phrase reading. If your child cannot yet read, he or she will still be able to tell when to turn the page by watching the pictures and listening to the music. Your child will get a great sense of achievement out of pretending to read song picture books.

Several companies publish high-quality tape recordings or records to accompany the books. It helps your preschooler learn to read by following along in a book while listening to a tape. Listening to a cassette while following along in the book is like being read to. Cassettes are especially fun to bring along on long car trips.

Song picture books come with a wide variety of songs spanning a rather wide age range. If you have a preschooler, you may want to choose lullabies, nursery rhymes, counting rhymes, and alphabet songs. All ages enjoy holiday songs and silly songs. If your child is older, try folk songs and historical songs. A few examples appear below.

Lullabies:
Aliki. *Hush Little Baby.* Englewood Cliffs, N.J.: Prentice-Hall, 1974.

Nursery rhymes:
Spier, Peter. *London Bridge Is Falling Down.* New York: Doubleday, 1967.
Stanley, Diane. *Fiddle-I-Fee: A Traditional American Chant.* Boston: Little, Brown, 1979.
Zuromskis, Diane. *The Farmer in the Dell.* Boston: Little, Brown, 1978.

Counting Rhymes:
Adams, Pam. *This Old Man.* New York: Grossett and Dunlap, 1975.
Keats, Ezra Jack. *Over in the Meadow.* New York: Four Winds Press, 1971.
Peek, Marie. *Roll Over! A Counting Song.* New York: Houghton Mifflin, 1981.

Alphabet Songs:
Provensen, Alice, and Martin Provensen. *A Peaceable Kingdom: The Shaker Abecedarius.* New York: Viking, 1978.
Yolen, Jane. *All in the Woodland Early: An ABC Book.* Illustrated by Jane Breskin Zalben. Cleveland: Collins-World, 1979.

Holiday Songs:

Child, Lydia M. *Over the River and Through the Wood.* Illustrated by Brinton Turkle. New York: Coward, McCann and Geoghegan, 1974.

Jeffers, Susan. *Silent Night.* Verse by Joseph Mohr. New York: E.P. Dutton, 1984.

Knight, Hilary. *Hilary Knight's the Twelve Days of Christmas.* New York: Macmillan, 1981.

Children enjoy reading historical markers when they visit parks and historical sites.

Historical Songs:

Spier, Peter. *The Erie Canal.* New York: Doubleday, 1970. The towpath for much of the length of the Erie Canal in central New York is now a hiking and bicycling trail. Children enjoy visiting parks along the canal which was the inspiration for the song.

Langstaff, John. *Ol' Dan Tucker.* New York: Harcourt Brace and World, 1963.

Quackenbush, Robert. *Skip to My Lou.* Philadelphia: Lippincott, 1975.

    Because of the popularity of song picture books, you can find many in paperback editions. You may want to compare two different versions of the same song. You and your child could make a song picture book as a gift. Use the ones you like best as models.

Often singing can lead to playing a musical instrument. There are children's books about musical instruments and the famous people who have played them well. A few examples are:
Isadora, Rachel. *Ben's Trumpet*. New York: Greenwillow, 1979.
Kuskin, Karla. *The Philharmonic Gets Dressed*. New York: Harper & Row, 1982.

If your child grows up in a musical family, he's likely to become a singer and musician. If your child grows up surrounded by books, he'll likely become an avid reader. The world of music offers many opportunities to learn how to read and to acquire rather advanced reading comprehension skills.

Following Directions

Have you ever baked a cake that didn't rise because you failed to include the baking powder, or have you ever assembled a kite that wouldn't fly? Many experiences in life require following directions. Businesses claim that they lose millions of dollars a year because their employees cannot follow written directions. We need to fill out forms accurately. Auto mechanics follow directions for installing new parts, repair workers follow manuals, teachers follow teacher's guides, and druggists follow prescriptions. Following directions, then, is an integral part of American life, and it is something children can practice as well.

When your child wants to make something, you can work on following directions. You can get ideas for making things from *Highlights for Children,* which includes a craft section each month where children can follow directions to make things. Your child might enjoy a hobby that involves making things and reading directions. For example, there are how-to books on knitting and sewing, gardening, magic, model making, photography, coin collecting, aquariums, origami, and raising pets. Virtually any activity your child is involved in has "how-to" books that give directions.

If your child belongs to a 4-H Club, Girl Scouts, or Boy Scouts, he or she will learn to follow written directions for entering contests or completing badges. Scouts keep written records of the cookies they sell and the activities they complete.

Following written directions is an important skill children will need all through their lives.

When your child follows directions, he or she has to read details and read in sequence. Reading directions is not as superficial as reading a novel can be. The concept of cause and effect becomes obvious.

Have you ever created a scavenger hunt for children? They seek out a treasure at the end of the hunt from clues you've dispersed in an orderly fashion around the house or yard. For example, one parent wrote out clues for a Valentine hunt, such as: "Sarah, Sarah, we love you. Look in the dollhouse for your next clue." Sarah had a wonderful time reading the rhymes and finding more clues to her Valentine.

Some parents post written directions for routine activities as a checklist for children. In a house I visited recently there was a sign on the bathroom door for the children:

1. Did you flush?
2. Did you rinse out the sink?
3. Did you hang up the bath mat?
4. Did you fold your towel?
5. Did you take all your belongings with you?

Thanks. I appreciate your help.
               Mom

Another family recently acquired a puppy. To housebreak

Growing Up Reading

him, the parents made a checklist including the names of each family member who would walk the new puppy every half hour.

Job checklists furnish daily reading activities as well as daily reminders of tasks to be performed.

Such checklists work well as reminders of daily tasks. When you are away, you can leave notes containing directions for starting supper or calling you on the telephone.

Your children will enjoy following directions if you provide the opportunities through invented games with written clues or as an accompaniment to hobbies and daily activities. Reading directions is an important reading skill to acquire.

Writing and Reading

Many children who are good readers are not good writers, but most children who write well are also good readers. Many of the thought processes involved in understanding reading can be learned by writing.

Your young child learns a lot from watching you write. He or she watches you write from left to right across a page and learns how the alphabet letters are formed. You can write messages, simple rhymes, and songs on a chalkboard or memo board for your children to try to read. Label photograph albums, and make books for and with your child. If you write personal letters and greeting cards, you'll receive a response, which can be posted on a bulletin board.

Young children learn a great deal about letters, words, and messages as they watch adults write.

There are many ways that you can provide writing experiences for young children. You can write for very young children long before the children themselves are able to write. You can write messages to accompany scribble pictures as gifts for family members or as greeting cards on holidays. When children are in the "naming of scribbling" and early drawing stages of art development, they typically request labels for their work.

Another way to write for children is to write notes to them and leave messages on the blackboard or memo board. Even though your child may not be able to read these immediately, he or she can ask for interpretations and, if the messages are short, will memorize the text and be able to read it at a later time. If any word is repeated frequently enough, such as the name of a family member or friend, your child will begin to recognize that word by sight.

When your child knows what the messages say, he or she will associate learning to read with receiving a message. That concept cannot be emphasized enough. Frequently, school instruction so focuses upon the form of language—the letters

Growing Up Reading 115

and how they sound and are blended together—that children forget momentarily that reading must make sense. Have you ever heard a child who is just learning how to read call out words with no apparent evidence that he is getting any meaning from them? A child might read the text, "The dog barked at the squirrel," as "The dog baked at the squirrel," and go right on with his or her "reading." The child who has learned that reading must contain a message would immediately see that no dog bakes and go back to correct the error.

Taking Dictation from Children
Even very young children can dictate messages for greeting cards and letters, labels for photograph albums, and messages for family members. As you are writing for your child, it is helpful if you sit side by side, rather than facing him or her, so that the left-right direction of writing is obvious and so that the letters that are produced come out right side up for the child. It is also helpful to spell the words as you are writing and to read the message at the end, pointing to the words as you read them. After a time, your child will learn to pace the dictation to the speed at which you are writing. This is the beginning of

Dictating to an adult enables a child to record stories too long for him to write.

matching speech to print, a very important reading-readiness skill.

You may find that your child enjoys coloring or tracing over the letters you have written. If you type, your child will enjoy playing at the typewriter. Play with written language can serve many functions. It clearly helps children develop concepts about words and about the formation of alphabet letters.

Once your child can write six or more letters of the alphabet it is time to stop being a secretary and to encourage the child to write independently. You don't want your child to depend on you for all writing tasks. You'll be surprised at the readable messages your child will be able to write after learning to form just a few consonants.

Even as they begin to learn how to write, youngsters have difficulty writing out the long stories they might be able to tell. You might want to sit at a typewriter and type out stories your child tells.

Children's Independent Writing

When young children write without your help, they are forced to think about how writing looks. They create their own symbols for letters, which we call mock letters ([? ∧ ⌯ ⊘). They have to invent spellings, and in doing so, begin to think about the characteristics of written words.

Children who are encouraged to write make signs and

Independent writers will make signs and labels part of their play.

labels to accompany their play. If you provide youngsters with paper and markers or other writing tools, they will write invitations to shows, provide tickets and programs, and even make door prizes! There is no end to children's creative uses of writing during play.

One way to link reading and writing is to write to the authors of favorite books. Many authors send a personal response. Does your community offer book fairs? Children's book authors give talks and autograph books for people at most book fairs.

A second link between reading and writing is when children become published authors themselves. A surprising number of children's magazines and even some adult newspapers accept children's writing. Some even pay children for it. The acceptance rate is probably no greater than it is for adults, and the children may collect many rejection slips en route to becoming published authors, but once their writing appears in print, the hard work and patience will have paid off.

Here are two books which might give your child some writing ideas:

Bernstein, Joanne E. *Fiddle with a Riddle: Write Your Own Riddles.*
   Illustrated by Giulio Maestro. New York: E. P. Dutton, 1979.
Morrison, Bill. *Squeeze a Sneeze.* Boston: Houghton Mifflin, 1977.

Television

Television sets are found in 98 percent of our homes. The TV sets in American households are turned on an average of six hours and forty-five minutes per day, and longer in households with children, according to a Neilson study. The impact of television upon children cannot be ignored.

Many things need to be considered when looking at the impact of television upon children. One is the alternatives. When children are watching television, what else might they be doing? Reading? Interacting with their parents? When compared with virtually any other type of activity, TV viewing falls short on benefits to children. The best advice, then, except for when there are special programs and special circumstances which will be discussed later, is to TURN THE TELEVISION OFF!

Occasionally, TV will stimulate a child to read a book. There are, unfortunately, too few literary television shows. However, when parents take an active role in their children's television viewing habits, they can turn what would normally be a negative experience into a positive one.

A program for children focusing directly on reading is "Reading Rainbow." This show shares quality children's books with its audience by having famous personalities read the stories. Host LeVar Burton discusses the books and shows activities which relate to the book.

PBS invites children to discover the magic world of books and reading on "Reading Rainbow."

Growing Up Reading

Help your children gain control over the amount of television and types of programs they watch. Then, with your help, they can use their televiewing to aid their critical-reading (and thinking) skills and to extend their reading habits.

Specifically, some television shows broaden children's experiences, giving them more background to bring to reading. For example, your children probably have never been to China, seen a polar bear, or observed a spaceship launch. Through television they can see all of these. Although the secondary television experience is much less effective than first-hand experience, it can still be beneficial.

In some cases, particularly in nature and science, television zoom lenses and X-ray photography provide pictures of things that could not be seen with the naked eye.

In addition, different types of television shows have the potential to stimulate reading in different ways.

Cartoons and Comedies
If your child enjoys comedy shows he might read funny books, humorous stories, and joke books. There are cartoon books available in bookstores. A favorite is *Never Tickle a Turtle: Cartoons, Riddles and Funny Stories,* by Mike Thaler (Franklin Watts, 1977).

You can encourage your child to collect favorite riddles and jokes into a book of his own. At holiday times he might enjoy reading funny greeting cards, such as "knock-knock" Valentines. Along with reading jokes, you can invent your own. Older children can identify forms of humor in the books they read and in the television shows they watch. There are essentially four types of humor to watch for:
1. Verbal—the manipulation of language in such ways as to create plays on words, puns, jokes, or sarcasm.
2. Human predicament—a situation in which someone appears foolish or suffers momentary misfortune.
3. Absurdity—ridiculous humor totally lacking in reason.
4. Incongruity—subtle humor that associates recognized incompatibilities.

Bill Peet is one of the most prolific writers of humorous books for children. Some of his titles include *Buford the Little Bighorn* (Houghton Mifflin, 1967), *The Wump World* (Houghton

Mifflin, 1970), and *Big Bad Bruce* (Houghton Mifflin, 1977). Other popular funny books include any of the "Amelia Bedelia" books by Peggy Parish (Greenwillow), *Animals Should Definitely Not Wear Clothing* by Judith Barrett (Atheneum, 1970), *A Treeful of Pigs* (Greenwillow, 1979), the *Frog and Toad* books by Arnold Lobel (Harper & Row), and *Because the Bug Went Ka-choo!* by Rosetta Stone (Random House, 1975). You can help your child compile his own lists of favorite funny books to enjoy with other children.

Here are several of a large number of riddle and joke books for children:

Aardema, Verna. *Ji-Nongo-Nongo Means Riddles.* Illustrated by Jerry Pinkney. New York: Four Winds Press, 1978.

Doty, Roy. *Tinkerbell's a Ding-a-ling.* New York: Doubleday, 1980.

Schwartz, Alvin. *Ten Copycats in a Boat and Other Riddles.* Illustrated by Marc Simont. New York: Harper & Row, 1980.

———. *Flapdoodle: Pure Nonsense from American Folklore.* Illustrated by John O'Brien. New York: J. B. Lippincott, 1980.

Young, Ed. *High on a Hill: A Book of Chinese Riddles.* New York: William Collins, 1980.

Adventure and Drama

You can enjoy adventure stories both on television and in books. Some books, such as *Snow Bound, Island of the Blue Dolphins, Ivanhoe,* and *Tom Sawyer,* have been made into movies and shown on television. The Walt Disney cable-television channel presents many adventures.

If your child enjoys watching drama, he or she might enjoy the books from which the television series were taken, such as *Little House on the Prairie.* In addition, try books by Carolyn Haywood, Robert McCloskey, and Maud Hart Lovelace. Or, for older children, Eleanor Estes, Sydney Taylor, Joan Blos, Charlotte Zolotow, Lois Lenski, Betsy Byars, and Julia Cunningham.

Science and Nature

On PBS, and occasionally on commercial television, science and nature shows are becoming more common ("Nova," "Jacques Cousteau," "Cosmos"). Children's programming—"Captain

Kangaroo" and "Mister Rogers"—practically always have some scientific content. "The New Zoo Review" and "3-2-1 Contact" feature animals and science. Children are fascinated by science. They develop a sense of wonder and a curiosity which spur them to investigate. If your child sees something interesting on TV, you can extend that interest through visits to planetariums, zoos, museums, and by reading some beautiful nonfiction science books. This is the area where the educational value of television pays great dividends. You can follow up on documentaries in newspapers and magazines about the event itself or in books about the scientific nature of the events in general.

Sports
There are an enormous number of sports shows on television. Many children enjoy watching these, especially if you are watching with them. Recently books for children have been published on chess, cycling, flying, hang gliding, gymnastics, hockey, tennis, horseback riding, kite making and flying, skating, surfing, swimming, diving, racquetball, baseball, lacrosse, backpacking, football, car racing, running, martial arts, baton twirling, frisbee throwing, soapbox derby racing, basketball, and track. In short, there are both television shows and current books on practically every sport you can name.

There is an equally impressive list of biographies of athletic stars from virtually all of these sports. Children tend to read and view athletic programs less passively than other types of programming, for there is an innate sense of drama in athletic accomplishments. Children can learn to identify those qualities in people that make them stars or leaders. They can write to athletic celebrities and will often receive responses. Your family might enjoy comparing the TV show of an athletic event to the written accounts in the next day's newspaper or the next week's sports magazine.

Mystery and Fantasy
Children's mystery programs and mystery books are popular with many children. It's fun to make a list of clues which might help solve the mysteries. Prediction is an important reading

skill, as are following events logically and looking for details. Your child might even enjoy writing his or her own mystery.

There are lots of fantasy shows on TV and in the movies ("Peter Pan," "Cinderella," "Star Wars," "Star Trek"). Most either come from children's books or are made into books after they appear on TV. Encourage your children to read the books and compare them with the TV versions. Why did the script writers select the parts they did for the film version?

Commercials

All children who watch television, unless they watch only public television, watch hours and hours of commercials. There are learning opportunities embedded even in commercials that can help children read better. Once children thoroughly understand that the intent of commercials is to persuade them to purchase products, they can examine the propaganda techniques used by commercials. Here are some:

> Bandwagon: Everybody loves eating Rayrays!
>
> Prestige: Mighty Mort, a champion gymnast, eats Rayrays.
>
> Testimonial: Superstar Lance LaRue says, "Rayrays are delicious."
>
> Plain folks: Down home in Middletown, we munch on Rayrays everyday.
>
> Snob appeal: Here on Capitol Hill, everyone adores eating Rayrays.
>
> Emotional appeal: Rayrays will make Mom proud of you. They are so good for you, and they taste good, too!
>
> Ego: Discriminating eaters chose Rayrays. How about you?
>
> Authority: More doctors recommend Rayrays because they're packed full of vitamins and minerals.
>
> Image: Champion tennis players eat Rayrays. You'll be just like them if you do, too.
>
> Oversimplification: You'll be happier if you eat Rayrays.

Growing Up Reading

Repetition: Rayrays, Rayrays, who wants some Rayrays?

If your child can figure out how a commercial is trying to sway him, chances are he'll be able to do the same thing with editorials and other persuasive writing he'll be reading.

These ideas are intended to show you that reading can, indeed, be found everywhere. It just takes a tiny bit of extra effort to include your children in these natural kinds of reading activities. The topics of cooking, shopping, traveling, music, following directions, writing, and television are intended only as examples of how reading is integral to daily life. Other topics (sewing, gardening, constructing, and playing) might have made this point equally well. Reading is everywhere, but only if you share it with your children will they benefit from it.

Chapter 6

Reading Strengths and Weaknesses

"That's the first book I've ever really read!"—12-year-old, after struggling through *The Great Gilly Hopkins* by Katherine Paterson.

"Jason doesn't read books, but you should see him follow directions to build model airplanes!"

There is an unfortunate tendency among many parents to compare their children to each other. These comparisons do a great disservice to children, who learn in myriad ways and at different rates. Parents who say, "Look at Johnny—he can sound out all those words, and my Mary can't even sound out her own name," may be unaware that Mary is a visual learner and probably never will do much sounding out as she reads. Yet she will read every bit as fluently as Johnny, and perhaps even more so.

Some children learn to read early, some late. In some cases, it is better for a child to learn to read at an older age because it is easier for him to learn then. In some schools where reading is not taught until children are eight years old, they learn more easily and there is less failure than in schools where reading is taught in kindergarten. While all parents would want to participate in informal reading activities with their children from birth on (as outlined in Chapter 1), it would be wrong to assume that all children will learn quickly. In the same way, it would be wrong to push preschoolers into formal reading programs for which they are not ready.

Observing Children

The best way to discover how your children learn is to observe them closely. Some children are active learners. They jump right into things. They take risks and attempt things beyond their capabilities. Other children are more cautious. They stand back until they have seen others do something, then carefully try it themselves. Some children learn best by observing others, while other children need to do things themselves in order to learn.

By observing what children learn easily, parents gain valuable information about their learning strengths.

You can make lists of what your children do well and what they have difficulty doing as a strategy for analyzing their learning styles. You get more positive results by building upon what your child can do well than by emphasizing weaknesses.

Some of us learn best by seeing, some by hearing, and some by touching and manipulating. By observing your children you'll discover what their modality strengths are. Modality refers to the primary sense an individual uses to learn and retain information. You might find that a child who has difficulty with phonics learns better through the kinesthetic mode of touching and feeling or the visual mode of seeing and watching, rather than the auditory mode necessary for listening to phonics instruction.

Does the child try to "sound out" words in the grocery store? Does the child handle all of the products while placing them in the cart? Does the child remember that soups are in the red and white cans next to the jellies? You can look for patterns of behavior to help determine modality preferences.

While reading aloud to her daughter, one parent noticed that her child's eyes were on the next page. When questioned about this behavior, the child replied, "To be honest, Mommy, I'm not listening." This child had such a strong visual preference that she read ahead and tuned out the oral reading.

Another child, after answering the telephone, was questioned by his parent, "Who was it?" The child answered, "I can't tell by voices, Mom. I have to tell by hair." This child was saying that his preference for learning is a visual, not an auditory, mode. This same child, when trying to learn his phone number said, "Oh, Dad, why don't you just write it down?" This child learned how to read primarily by memorizing sight words. His phonics skills came after he had become a fluent reader by sight methods.

One auditorily oriented child could memorize rhyme after rhyme after hearing them once. On his third birthday he exclaimed to all who would listen, "Look, I can say *water* now!" Up until that time his *w* sounds had come out *h*, and he had heard the difference and tried diligently to make the switch to the *w* sound. He was pleased with his accomplishment. His fire engines shrieked, the brakes squealed, and the water rushed out

There are lots of sound effects when an auditory child plays.

of the hose: all of his pretend play was noisy. He learned how to read by sounding out words. He read Dr. Seuss's *Hop on Pop* over and over as an early reading book.

His sister was visually oriented and learned to remember sight words. One day, when her mother was busy in the kitchen and could not respond to her pleas to come and read with her, she said in disgust, "Well, if you won't read to me, then I'll have to read it myself." And read it herself she did! She spelled out loud each word that she did not know. Her mother told her what the word was, and the child remembered it.

A third child is a kinesthetic learner. Mandi simply cannot sit still. She hugs everybody. She wiggles and moves when being read to. She insists on holding the book and turning the pages, even though with all of her wiggling it is hard to read the book. Mandi loves to draw and write words but is far less interested in

The visual child learns by sight, remembering words she has seen.

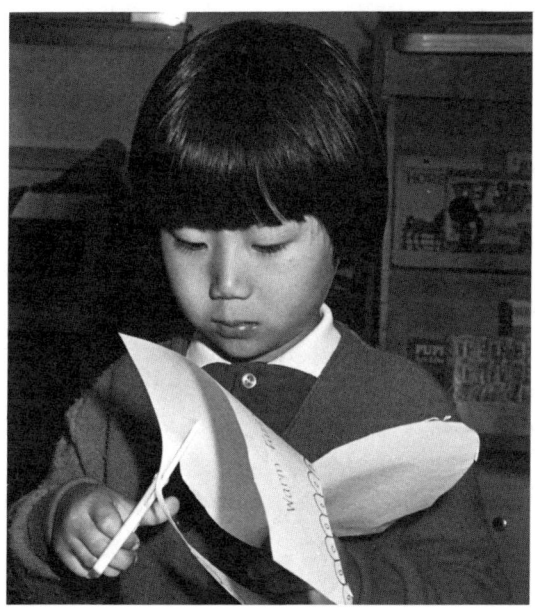

Constantly on the move, a kinesthetic learner loves to draw, write, and cut words out of paper.

Growing Up Reading

reading them. She can read words on cards she has traced with her finger but has difficulty with the same words in a book. Mandi cuts her words out of paper. She plays with manipulative letters to form words. Mandi loves puppets and often retells stories using puppets that she has made.

Learning to read was hard for Mandi, who had trouble sitting still long enough to read a selection. For Mandi reading instruction probably should have been delayed until she was older and had more concentration. It definitely needed to be presented kinesthetically with opportunities for her to take part physically in the process. Mandi would not respond well to worksheets or dittos nor to sitting still in reading groups.

If your child is having difficulty in learning something, you might determine if the learning is being presented in the child's preferred modality. If it isn't, you might suggest that another mode of instruction be used. If a child is having difficulty in school with one approach to reading, you might consider trying alternative approaches at home, instead of giving the child repeated drill on the same thing the child has difficulty with in school.

Building on a child's modality strengths gives the child the same privilege that adults have. We automatically use our modality strengths. If we are kinesthetically oriented, we prefer visiting the source of the news story. If we are visually oriented, we prefer either a newspaper or the television. If we are auditorily oriented, we listen to the radio for news or listen to television more than watch it. Children need to be given these choices as well. To confine learning to visual or auditory modes, as is so often done in school, is to deprive some children of their best opportunities for learning.

An excellent source of information on modality strengths is *Teaching Through Modality Strengths: Concepts and Practices*, by Walter B. Barbe, Ph.D., and Raymond Swassing (Zaner-Bloser, 1979).

Children Who Experience Difficulty Reading

We do not have absolute answers for why some children learn more easily than others, nor can we identify all of the causes for reading difficulties. Though they contribute to relatively few reading problems overall, physical factors are fairly easy to verify.

Psychological and Educational Factors
Reading disability is usually related to emotional problems of various sorts. Whether a psychological problem is the cause of a reading problem or the reading problem caused the psychological problem is often difficult to determine. Signs of developing problems might be exhibited by children who do not want to go to school or who avoid reading situations, especially in front of other people. Emotional problems are aggravated by parents who are demanding or critical or who push their children beyond their capabilities. Children who can never please their parents, no matter how hard they try, will quit trying.

If your child comes to school with feelings of self-doubt, he or she may be less able to take the risks necessary in learning to read and may become discouraged more easily than the happy, confident, secure child. Our society attaches so much importance to the act of reading that to fail causes a child's whole self-concept to become damaged. To fail at athletics, music, art, and even arithmetic is not considered so critical. This societal imbalance and emphasis upon reading needs to be countered by building up children's self-concepts in areas where they excel.

Intelligence is considered a determinant of reading potential. Typically, very bright children learn how to read rather easily; children with very low IQ scores have a difficult time learning to read. However, there are exceptions to these generalizations. And, in the large middle ranges of intelligence, reading is more related to other factors such as exposure to writing and the desire to read.

Children in small families typically receive more parental attention, are read to more often, and therefore acquire reading more easily than children who come from larger families. Children who come from middle or above-average income homes typically have access to more reading materials and therefore have a head start toward reading.

Children whose first language is not English often have

difficulty learning to read in English. Bilingual programs have been established to help make the transition from another language to English a smooth one for these children. Some of these programs treat English as a second language, as was done historically by many immigrants to this country. Other

Children who recieve bilingual instruction at an early age usually have no difficulty learning to read.

programs, however, strive to help children become totally bilingual, providing instruction in their native tongue parallel to instruction in English, with the goal of maintaining the first language. Children who receive this instruction early in life usually have no difficulty learning how to read. In fact, their second language acquisition process helps them in language skills. Children who are acquiring English as a second language at the same time they are learning how to read, however, should not be rushed into learning to read. They should not be learning to read words not yet in their oral vocabularies. Often, for these children, writing is a good entry into the world of print.

Children whose general physical health is poor may develop reading problems. These children tend to miss more school because of sickness, making it difficult for them to keep up with a group in sequential reading programs.

Occasionally, children have neurological problems. Some are caused by brain dysfunction and others are termed "dyslexia." Dyslexia is "severe reading disability for no apparent reason."

It is important not to label children in ways that will harm them for years to come. If a child is labeled "dyslexic," that child can be sent to special classes. While special help can be advantageous—even necessary, labeling is more often harmful than helpful.

Reading problems rarely fit into one category. Physical, psychological, and educational problems are often interrelated. And for that very reason, the solutions to these problems are not simple. Some problems are very difficult to diagnose—even specialists don't always know what is wrong.

The most important point to remember if you have children with reading problems is to be supportive and not critical of your children's efforts. Then, even if they learn more slowly than is typical, your children will grow up reading.

Visual Problems
The visually dyslexic child has difficulty processing language symbols in their proper order or sequence. This difficulty may also be reflected in the child's inability to name the days of the week, the months of the year, or the alphabet letters in their correct order.

Most children with visual problems tend to move their lips and whisper as they read.

Growing Up Reading

Virtually all children with visual problems *subvocalize* (move their lips and whisper) when they read. Allowing your child to subvocalize as he or she reads lets the child *hear* what he or she is reading. This can help the visual processing of information if it is deficient.

Characteristics of visual problems become evident when children try to copy adults' writing. While copying, they can't sustain their vision and therefore lose their place and work very slowly. They reverse alphabet letters and ignore punctuation and capitalization. There may be frequent misspellings and erasures because they see the writing differently each time they look at it.

Children with visual problems may also have difficulty with reading comprehension. They may have trouble following the sequence of a story, finding details, drawing inferences, or identifying main ideas.

If your child has visual problems it takes longer to learn to read, and it is a more difficult task than it is for the typical child. Therefore, the pace should be slowed down and the pressure for learning to read removed. Since much of the problem is seeing things in sequence, it is important to read aloud so that your child can hear the order of events in a story's plots.

Write down stories your child tells. Then he or she can remember a sequence he or she has experienced and not just heard about. The stories contain words your child has told you. Hearing the words helps the child remember them. Encourage your child to read out loud so he or she can hear what is read.

Drilling your child on reversal problems may prove frustrating, since it is emphasizing a weakness. Once the child learns to comprehend what he or she reads you don't want the focus to be on individual letters or even words. Good readers read phrases at a time. Their eyes jump across the page; they don't move smoothly. Your child's reading comprehension can be improved by writing. While writing, they are using reading comprehension skills—building a plot sequence and focusing on a main idea.

Help your children overcome their weaknesses by using alternative strategies (especially auditory and kinesthetic approaches). Help them get meaning from print and not focus on individual words. Don't drill them on vocabulary words in isolation. Encourage the use of context for figuring out the meanings of unfamiliar words.

Encourage your child to read punctuation marks orally and to spell out loud.

Auditory Problems

Auditory problems are similar to visual problems except that children are unable to easily process information they have heard that is helpful in learning to read. Children with auditory problems have trouble with spelling and phonics. They have difficulty rhyming or discovering words that start with similar sound patterns. Children with auditory problems have difficulty blending words into parts or sounds into words. Sometimes their pronunciation is garbled.

If your child has auditory difficulties, he or she needs additional repetition of information. You might read stories several times if your child is interested. Combining pictures or props with storytelling helps your child see a story progress. Flannel boards are ideal for this. Kinesthetic experiences are helpful for learning alphabet letters and their sounds. Your child might enjoy making words out of magnetic letters, playing with wooden and sandpaper letters, writing letters and words, and touching letters in other ways. When your child reads, he or she can point to words to give an added kinesthetic dimension to reading.

Playing with magnetic, wooden, or sandpaper letters can help a child learn alphabet letters and their sounds.

A child with auditory problems should be given the opportunity to learn to read primarily through visual means—by learning sight words. Your child might be able to memorize "key" words, favorite words that he or she wants to learn how to read. Most children learn to read before they learn to write, but children with auditory problems would probably do better if they learned to write first. The kinesthetic and visual learning modes are used more for writing than they are for reading and, thus, they may be able to compensate for the weaker auditory mode.

Help your child look at words and remember how they look, rather than encouraging him or her to sound them out. Wait until your child can spell a number of words by sight before showing him or her spelling patterns which apply to other similar words.

Hearing-impaired and profoundly deaf children who are read to (signed to) by their parents and have full access to print environments and language environments (via sign language) become fluent readers just as hearing children do.

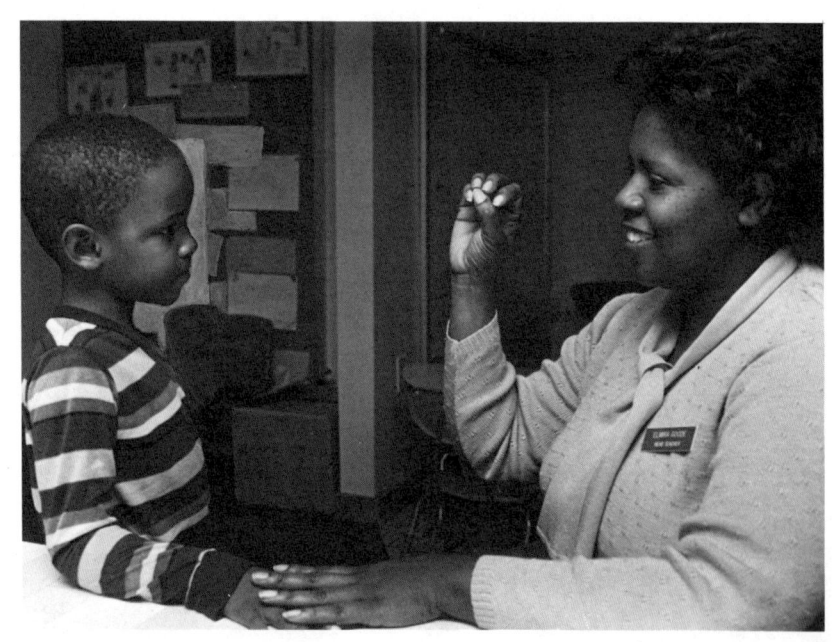

Hearing-impaired children become fluent readers when given the same reading opportunities as hearing children.

Dysgraphia

Dysgraphia describes children who can read but who have great difficulty with writing. Many children are careless in handwriting. All children reverse letters as they are learning to write and write from right to left at some point in their development. For children with persistent problems like these, however, writing will be very difficult. Their problems are perceptual in nature and involve motor impairments that make it very difficult for them to copy simple shapes and to form alphabet letters. These children can compose meaningful thoughts if they dictate their ideas and have someone else write them down, but their handwriting is so poor that they cannot get their own thoughts down on paper.

Often, children with dysgraphia exhibit mirror writing and write from right to left. They either omit letters or add them to words they are trying to spell. Their hand and arm muscles don't do what their head wants them to do. Even muscle exercises rarely produce measurable results.

Fortunately, in today's world, people can get by with very little handwriting. If your child has dysgraphia, give him a typewriter at the earliest possible moment. Work closely with your child's teacher so that moments of embarrassment are kept

The typewriter or computer keyboard can rescue a child with handwriting problems from undue embarrassment.

Growing Up Reading

at a minimum. Cursive handwriting may be easier than manuscript printing, since the pen stays on the paper and does not have to be brought up and down for each alphabet letter. Overall, however, the typewriter or computer keyboard with video screen and printer are the best solutions to severe handwriting problems.

Slow Readers

Some children, while not exhibiting a specific learning disability as described above, learn to read more slowly than other children. If they don't keep up with the class, they feel inferior to the rest of the children, become discouraged, and become failures. You may need to provide added assistance to your child if he takes longer to learn to read.

If your child is in the slowest reading group in class, for example, he or she needs more exposure to reading than is available in school. With slow reading groups teachers emphasize decoding skills, while faster reading groups are given more comprehension exercises. A child in the slower reading group needs additional opportunities to receive assistance that focuses on comprehension.

Several researchers have studied children in low-reading groups to see how they differ from children in the high-reading groups and then to use that information to design tutoring programs for remedial readers.

Children in low-reading groups think reading is a different process than high-group readers. As a result, their reading behaviors differ radically. Children in low-reading groups think that reading is: (1) getting the words right, (2) sounding them out, and (3) doing schoolwork. Children in the high-reading group perceive reading as: (1) a pleasurable, solitary activity, (2) a way to find out information, and (3) a socially acceptable thing to do.

Partially because of these radically different concepts of what reading is about, low readers behave differently when they read. Children who are good readers correct themselves; poor readers just continue to read, even if it makes no sense. Good readers concentrate on the meaning when they read. Poor readers concentrate on the sounds that the words make. Good readers use many strategies to read unfamiliar text. Poor readers use only one: sounding it out. Good readers reread passages in books and thus become very fluent readers. Poor readers seldom reread anything and thus never really become fluent readers. Good readers read a variety of things, while poor readers mainly read basal readers. Since children read differently in different kinds of material, the over-reliance on basals does not provide enough opportunities for qualitatively different reading.

These differences have implications for parents of children in low-reading groups.

(1) Read aloud to your child often and from a variety of materials to model fluent reading.
(2) Read aloud passages as a model before the child reads them.
(3) When your child is reading, don't make corrections or provide unknown words, but allow the child to finish the sentence and then self correct. Then if no correction is made, ask, "Does that make sense to you?"
(4) Don't say, "Sound it out."
(5) Let your child reread stories and passages until he reads them fluently. Then provide more audiences for him to read to, such as a younger child, a parent, or a tape recorder. Allow your child to build confidence in himself as a reader. When poor readers begin to think of reading and to behave the way good readers do, their reading skills will improve dramatically.

Many parents have the misguided notion that their children should be constantly challenged with "hard" books. In public libraries you can hear parents tell their children, "Don't get that book—it's too easy for you." Parents will purchase difficult books for slow readers or poor readers, thinking that these books will help their children become better readers. Actually, fluency at any level of skill acquisition—whether playing a piano or reading—is a result of lots of practice at that level and review at previous levels prior to moving on to a more difficult level.

Most children who are slow at learning can learn to read very successfully. They just need a longer time to master what other children are picking up rather quickly. They need more exposure to print and more time with paper and pencil. They need to feel at ease and not pressured by learning. Given the time that they need and supportive adults to help them, almost all children can grow into reading gracefully.

Children Who Read Early

Children who read early generally maintain that lead until at least upper elementary school. Early readers become better spellers and better at reading school assignments. The fact that early readers have a head start in school has caused some parents to push their children into reading too soon. This is detrimental to parent/child relationships. Some children pick up reading rather easily. These are the ones who maintain the lead and enjoy reading. Parents who push their children into reading may find that their children experience difficulty later and shy away from reading. These children won't develop a reading habit, making their parents' push counterproductive in the long run.

Children who read early are different in one way from their peers. Your child may try to camouflage that difference by hiding his or her reading ability or requesting to do work like the other children. You can help your child feel good about being different by pointing out how each child is special. Encourage your child to help other children, and provide opportunities for him or her to share the special talent—perhaps by reading aloud to a younger sibling.

It is important not to ignore early reading ability. Your child is obviously successful at reading and is ready and eager to learn more. To simply leave reading out of his or her day is to ignore that activity he or she enjoys the most.

Don't be surprised if your child, who is reading thick books at home, reverts back to reading picture books and shorter books at school. In school, learning usually takes place in short time blocks or at least in time periods that feel short to a child who has sat for an hour and read a book without interruption. One way to adapt to these shorter time blocks is by selecting shorter books that he or she can complete in one sitting.

Some parents of early readers have been encouraged to have their child skip a grade. For some mature children, this may be a good idea. But, for most, school is a social as well as an educational experience. Children who are placed ahead miss many informal social learning opportunities with their peers. If you are considering placing your child ahead, be sure to consider how he or she might feel to be the youngest child in the class each year.

Choosing Challenging Books
There are a great many books for poor readers who need mature content. There are books about sports heroes, mysteries, and science-fiction series, all written with controlled vocabularies and simple story lines.

Your mature reader, on the other hand, needs books that are just the opposite—books with longer, more complex sentences, with advanced vocabularies, and little repetition. But it can be hard to find challenging books that are not too sophisticated.

One solution is to seek out books that were written a number of years ago. Such books were relatively free of violence and sex. They were often sexist, but that can be discussed while your child is reading the book. Older books have challenging vocabularies and, at the same time, are likely to have good stories since they have been popular in the library for so many years! Two authors very popular among older readers are Carolyn Haywood, who wrote *"B" is for Betsy* (Harcourt Brace, 1939) and the Eddie Books, and Maud Hart Lovelace, whose Betsy-Tacy books have been reprinted as paperbacks.

Books about other cultures have specialized vocabularies unique to each culture. These books are usually different enough to be challenging and interesting, yet simple enough for young children to enjoy. One of the best authors of this type of book is Lois Lenski, whose tales of other American cultures include *Strawberry Girl* (Lippincott, 1945), *Shoo-Fly Girl* (Lippincott, 1963), and many others.

Your advanced reader can move on to other types of literature since he or she is not so dependent upon pictures as average readers might be. Poetry collections are real favorites. Poetry is challenging to read because poems include word play, imagery, and other writing techniques. Much poetry for children is humorous, so it is highly entertaining. Plays,

Books by Lois Lenski provide children with accurate insights into different American cultures.

nonfiction, biographies, and folk literature are other types of books for mature readers.

As your child gets older, he or she can delve into the classics that are normally reserved for middle-school or high-school readers. Unabridged versions are appropriate.

Resources

Where can you turn for information about the gifted and for ideas for stimulating your child? A particularly good source of information comes from Resources for the Gifted, Inc., 3421 North 44th Street, Phoenix, AZ 85018. You provide your child with a lifetime of problem-solving tools when you teach him or her the most basic skill of all—how to think. The materials published by Resources for the Gifted do just that.

Many books and materials are being published for the parents of gifted children. There is *Gifted Children Newsletter* published twelve times a year by Gifted and Talented Publications, Inc., P.O. Box 115, Sewell, NJ 08080.

Other recommended sources are:
Everyday Enrichment
National/State Leadership Training Institute
 on the Gifted and the Talented
Civic Center Tower Building
316 West Second Street, Suite P4-C
Los Angeles, CA 90012

Thinking Cap
Box 7239
Phoenix, AZ 85001

If you have questions about the education of the gifted, inquire at your local college or university to find up-to-date information and resources.

Every Child Is Gifted

Not all early readers are gifted and not all gifted children are early readers. In fact, every child is gifted, and you, as a parent

Children exhibit a variety of physical and intellectual gifts. It's our job to build upon those gifts.

need to observe carefully to determine each child's gifts and to capitalize on them. Children who are gifted in reading are not always gifted at math; children who have early mathematical success are not always early readers. Children who exhibit physical gifts, such as throwing, running, and jumping, do not always exhibit intellectual gifts. No matter what gifts children have, it is important to build upon them and not waste their natural human talents.

Chapter 7

Maintaining Reading Habits

"**I** can't come Sunday—that's when we go to the library."
"My magazine came today? Oh goody!"
"I sure hope I can find another Beverly Cleary book."

There are vast numbers of people in our society who have the ability to read but who seldom read anything at all. Yet a person who does not read is just as poorly informed as a person who cannot read. Schools have as their goal for instruction that every child should learn how to read. Rarely do schools go beyond teaching children how to read, to helping them develop the reading habit.

People who read are seldom bored. Reading helps people become well-informed. There is some evidence that people who read are more content in their retirement years. It is amazing that over half of our population receives all of its information about world events, including information on which candidates to vote for, solely by watching television!

Studies show that if adults do not read, their ability to read atrophies. Without practice, we lose vocabulary and comprehension skills which we had while in school. With economic and social events becoming far more complex, more sophisticated reading skills are needed for a person to be a literate member of society. Democracies depend upon an educated electorate for their very existence. It is up to you, as a parent, to provide opportunities for the development of reading habits.

Developing Routine Reading Times

Children most easily develop the reading habit when they have routine times for reading. The most common time many families find they can put aside for reading is just before bed. After reading aloud, some families allow their children fifteen minutes more time to read and look at books before lights go out. Reading settles children down before they go to sleep and helps reduce the tension of the day.

More than any other routine, the bedtime reading habit helps children become addicted to reading.

Children who have developed this habit have been known to take a book with them on "sleep overs" or slumber parties. The book becomes as necessary a part of the bedtime routine as the toothbrush.

Other family traditions that make reading habitual include keeping books to read in the car. Many families with young children take a few books with them everywhere, so that if they have to wait in a traffic jam or in a restaurant or in a business office, their children always have something to do. Children who have been raised to have a book handy all the time develop the habit of taking some reading material with them for those inevitable waiting times that occur regularly in our lives.

Developing the Library Habit

Have you visited your public library lately? Libraries are a far cry from what they used to be twenty or even ten years ago. Today's libraries are interesting places with a wide range of materials and services for children and parents. Public libraries serve the public and are responsive to parents' suggestions. Most libraries have support groups that generate interest in projects and solicit funds as well.

Programs for Infants and Toddlers
Many libraries have programs for the parents of infants. Some libraries offer classes during the day that allow you to bring your baby and try exercises, songs, stories, and games with your baby. Other libraries hold night meetings, sometimes with babysitting available, where you can learn up-to-date information about raising children.

Toddler programs are more structured and are for parents of children between the ages of eighteen months and two years. Librarians read stories, show filmstrips, do puppet shows, flannel-board stories, or in other ways get children involved. Your toddler sits on your lap during the sessions, and you participate as well. In some programs, each toddler borrows a couple of paperback books to be returned the following week. Parents are provided with lists of related books and the words to the fingerplays or songs from the session. You can provide continuity between sessions as your children are learning new rhymes and stories.

Unfortunately, with library cutbacks, infant and toddler programs are some of the first to go. But if you find these programs useful, you can organize to rally support and funding for them.

Programs for Preschoolers
Preschoolers are the traditional group for whom story hours were designed. At about the age of three children become willing and able to leave their parents for an hour to attend an interesting story session. These sessions often include story reading, films or filmstrips, flannel boards, puppet shows, songs, dances, finger plays, storytelling, or even crafts related

to stories or themes. Some librarians encourage the children to bring their teddy bears or dolls for a pajama story hour.

Some libraries have branched out from preschool programs to include programs which appeal to a wider age range for special holidays—spooky stories at Halloween, Christmas

Librarians are often masterful storytellers who encourage children to participate during story hour.

holiday parties, and spring frolics are examples. Some libraries offer pajama story hours for children to which all members of the family are welcome.

Programs for School-Age Children
Some libraries provide regular after-school story hours. They also offer programs children can participate in independently, such as reading contests and book fairs.

Library Visits as Family Routines
Whether your children can participate in library programs or not, you want to be sure that they make regular visits to the library. Set aside an hour on Sunday afternoon or one night each week for your family to routinely visit the library. Regular library visits stimulate reading. They expose your family to a

wide range of reading materials, and they give your children regular opportunities to talk about books with enthusiastic readers outside the family. Librarians are also very helpful in making book recommendations. Knowing that there is a deadline when books need to be returned encourages children to read at home so they can finish the books before they are due back at the library. Children who visit the library weekly become more discriminating readers through exposure to a wider variety of literature than is available in most homes. By selecting their own books, children learn to reject some and consider others. Library routines, such as checking out their own books and returning them on time, help develop responsibility in children.

Checking out books and returning them on time help children develop responsibility and establish familiar library routines.

Bookmobiles
What is important in each of these library programs is that your child learns to make the library a part of his regular weekly routine. Once children become readers, they need a readily available source of new books. Often a bookmobile is closer to home and more convenient than the public library. Many public

libraries were built in the old downtown sections of cities that are now difficult and time-consuming to reach. Bookmobiles travel to shopping centers, taking the library to its customers. The bookmobile has a number of advantages over the library. It

Equipped with popular books and staff members who can provide personal service, bookmobiles help promote the library habit.

is smaller and less intimidating. The staff can be more personal because they get to know their regular customers well. Bookmobile staff members can bring special orders with them from the main library the following week. Because bookmobiles have fewer books, there is variety in a small space. Children, who in the public library might go only to the picture book section or the fiction section, find other types of books to choose from. Poetry, nonfiction, adventures, and mysteries are shelved right next to the popularly read children's books. Bookmobiles are stocked with the most popular books, providing an almost guaranteed selection of good books.

Bookmobiles have one big disadvantage: a limited offering. They are a great place to go just to find reading material, but if you have a question you want answered or are looking for books on specific topics, a trip to the library itself might be in order.

Library Reference Resources
Is your child full of questions that you can't answer? Once he or she has learned the alphabet, he or she can learn to find things

out by using indexes, reference books, and the card catalog. A good way to learn these skills is with a children's dictionary. You can play games to see who can find a word faster, you in an adult dictionary or your child using a children's dictionary. The key to using any resource is being able to look things up quickly.

Point out guide words in the dictionary. Children rapidly learn whether to open the dictionary to the beginning, the middle, or the end as they recognize the first letter of the word they are seeking.

A library usually has several encyclopedia sets. When your children are studying certain topics in school, they can look up the topics in an encyclopedia to answer questions and find more information.

One of the most exciting things to learn about is the card catalog. After your child has enjoyed a book by a particular author, look in the card catalog to see if the library has other books by the same person. After enjoying books on a certain topic, see if there are others on that subject. Sometimes a teacher, librarian, or relative will recommend a book to a child. He or she can look in the card catalog to find out if the library has the book and, if so, where it is.

Going from the card catalog to the bookshelves is another learning experience for children. Fiction books are shelved

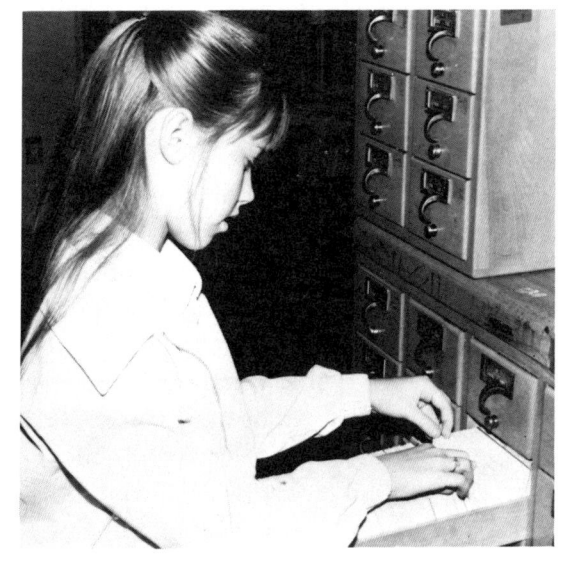

Children quickly learn to use the card catalog to find out about different books and where they are located.

alphabetically by the author's last name. If you and your child have used the library a lot together, your child can probably tell you where books by certain authors are located. Using these familiar spots as reference points, you can branch out to finding books by favorite authors, using the alphabetical listing by author's name. Studies show that children who seek out books by author are better readers and more avid readers than children who do not notice the authors of the books they read. For nonfiction books, you'll use the Dewey Decimal System or Library of Congress numerical coding systems. In practice, however, your child soon learns where the biographies, poetry, and plays are kept and can find those sections quickly.

Many libraries are hooked up to larger regional library systems for interlibrary loan purposes. That makes it easier for you to get books that have been recommended but are not available in your local libraries. It used to be terribly frustrating to read the review of a good book and then be unable to get a copy except by ordering it in a local bookstore. Now, most people are within range of a rather exhaustive library, and with the use of interlibrary loan systems, they have access to a wide variety of children's books.

There are so many questions that arise in the course of a day that might be explored in the library. If your children get into the habit of going to the library to seek answers to their questions, their own curiosity will sustain their reading habits.

Library Services
Libraries have quite a few materials other than books that can be used in the library and, in some cases, checked out. Most libraries have interesting displays and collections. They have peephole dioramas, museum collections, rotating specialized displays, fish, gerbils, and other animals for children to observe.

Most libraries have book-related media, such as children's records, filmstrips, cassettes, and movies. You can borrow the equipment just as you would books. If these materials can't be checked out of your library, at least they can be used there. Your child might enjoy looking at filmstrips of favorite books. Experiencing a book in a variety of media makes children more familiar with the story.

Many libraries offer interesting displays, such as peephole dioramas, for children to observe.

In larger cities there are more advanced facilities. You can dial a story on the telephone, call for information to be gathered, or listen to a talk. Computers have revolutionized people's access to resources. It is possible that in the future you may be able to check out books from the library, using your home computer.

Public libraries, then, provide families with many useful services. Children who are well-acquainted with their public libraries will be more likely to use the library as a source of information and recreation. Those habits will support reading well beyond the school years.

School Libraries

Most schools today have libraries (or media centers) even if they are unable to provide a full-time librarian for instructing and advising the children. Children who regularly visit a school library develop a library habit that can be transferred to the public library at any age.

Some teachers send books home and ask parents to read aloud to their children. Parental reading has been found to contribute to higher scores on standardized tests at the end of the school year.

When your children take books out of the school library, they need to be responsible for returning the books on time.

Therefore, books need to be stored carefully. You might have a special library shelf or book box where library books are kept separate from your family's books. You might also write scheduled library visits on your family's activity calendar.

Children's Magazines

Another type of recreational reading both children and adults enjoy is magazine reading. Both magazines and newspapers inform and entertain. You have to take what is offered on TV, but you can select from a much broader range of periodical publications. If your child learns to enjoy reading magazines now, he or she will likely retain that habit into adulthood.

There are a number of excellent publications for children. They are a very economical way to provide regular reading material. One magazine subscription costs as much as one or at the most two children's books. Yet there are usually between eight and twelve issues of a magazine each year. Each magazine contains a wider variety of reading material than a book would. Subscriptions make excellent gifts for children, especially from busy adults or people who find shopping difficult. They provide a whole year of enjoyment and can be ordered easily from your home.

There are two different types of magazines for children: all-purpose magazines, which include everything from stories and poems on a wide variety of topics to games and puzzles; and specialized magazines dealing with one area of study, such as science or social studies. With so many children's magazines available, it can be difficult to decide which are the best to purchase. Since your library subscribes to children's magazines, you might see which ones your child most enjoys reading there. It is always a good idea to write for sample copies of the magazines.

Your children will enjoy receiving their own magazines in the mail. Store their magazines with your adult publications so that they are read in the living room or family room along with adults. When you throw away your magazines, though, don't throw away the children's magazines. Your children will reread old issues if you keep them available on a bookshelf. Old magazines make excellent reading materials for long car trips.

In addition to subscribing to children's magazines, you can find collections of them at garage sales. Schools appreciate donations of used children's magazines when your children have outgrown them.

Some excellent publications for children are listed below:

Cricket
P.O. Box 100
LaSalle, IL 61301

Cricket publishes stories written by famous children's authors and illustrated by well-known artists for elementary school children. Some of the stories are a bit heavy for younger readers; some can be read aloud for family sharing. There are puzzles, contests, and letters to the editor. When your child writes to *Cricket* he'll get a clever postcard response.

Highlights for Children
803 Church Street
Honesdale, PA 18431

Highlights is just about the only all-purpose publication for children from two to twelve. Its regular features have remained popular since it was first published in 1946. Stories are on a wide range of topics. Craft ideas, games, puzzles, word fun, and learning activities fill its pages. The motto of *Highlights* is "Fun with a Purpose," suggesting an educational bent to its recreational reading material.

Your Big Backyard
National Wildlife Federation
1412 16th Street NW
Washington, DC 20036

The photographs in *Your Big Backyard* alone are worth the investment in this magazine, which comes once a month for children from one year to preschool age. The articles are short, interesting, and beautifully illustrated. The games are simple yet thought-provoking. There is a related activity in each issue.

Ranger Rick
National Wildlife Federation
1412 16th Street NW
Washington, DC 20036

Also published by the National Wildlife Federation, *Ranger Rick* is for children between the ages of six and twelve. The photographs are excellent and the information accurate.

> *Chickadee* and *Owl*
> Young Naturalist Foundation
> 51 Front Street E
> Toronto, Ontario M5E 1B3 Canada

Chickadee is for children between the ages of four and eight, and *Owl* is for children between eight and fourteen. Both publications offer excellent photographs and outstanding illustrations in every issue. The articles are informative and well written, and the games, puzzles, and activities offer young readers a variety of features to enjoy.

> *National Geographic World*
> 17th and M Streets NW
> Washington, DC 20036

World is oriented toward nature and science. The content and illustrations are superb. *World* is a bit more challenging than *Ranger Rick*, so might be kept for slightly older children.

> *Ebony Jr.*
> 820 South Michigan Avenue
> Chicago, IL 60605

Ebony Jr. is for children, especially black children, ages six to twelve.

> *Odyssey*
> 625 E. St. Paul Ave.
> Milwaukee, WI 53202

Concepts that might seem difficult at first are made interesting and accessible to children through an excellent blend of photography and illustration. Focusing on astronomy and outer space, *Odyssey* periodically includes special contests and Science Fair projects in addition to its regular features.

> *Cobblestone*
> 20 Grove St.
> Peterborough, NH 03458

Cobblestone is a history magazine that the entire family will enjoy. Each issue focuses upon a theme or topic, such as immigration, black history, or the Civil War. There are child-involvement departments—letters to the editor, recipes, and puzzles.

Classical Calliope
20 Grove St.
Peterborough, NH 03458

This magazine contains "the classics" in literature for children between the ages of ten and seventeen.

Faces
20 Grove St.
Peterborough, NH 03458

Faces is written in cooperation with the American Museum of Natural History. It is about people from all over the world, for children ages eight to fourteen.

Penny Power
256 Washington Street
Mount Vernon, NY 10053

Because children are consumers, too, this magazine is a youthful version of *Consumer Reports*. It teaches children to be cautious buyers and contains interesting analyses of products they might buy.

A magazine written *by children* is:
Stone Soup
Children's Art Foundation
P.O. Box 83
Santa Cruz, CA 95063

Your child will enjoy several magazine subscriptions. If a magazine is not being read, the subscription can be cancelled. Either the magazine is too old for your child (and can be reinstated at a later time), he or she has outgrown it, or he or she is not interested in the content. You might consider making your children chip in financially to support their magazine subscriptions. That is a good test of the magazine's worth.

Purchasing Books

Your child is far more likely to be an avid reader if he or she has a large collection of good books at home. Finding good books can be a challenge. To get the books you want, you may have to special-order them. Bookstores usually have a current listing of *Books in Print*, so they can find the publisher and ordering information for any book in print. All you need is the title of a book for a bookstore to order it for you. Most stores will make special orders, though some add on a small service charge for doing so.

Books make wonderful gifts. Children especially enjoy receiving books of their very own. Paperback books are more readily available; hardbound books are more costly. There is a big difference between a paperback and a hardbound book, however. Paperback books will not withstand the test of time, especially in warm and humid climates. And there is something special about owning a hardbound that the paperback cannot replicate. You need both kinds of books. Children could not have a very extensive library without collecting paperback books, but they would miss not having favorite books in hardbound volumes.

Most children's bookstores sell paperback books. One family enjoys spending Friday evenings at a bookstore. They tell their child that she may purchase one paperback book and she spends the evening reading many to decide on the best purchase.

Most children's bookstores make paperback as well as hardbound books available to young readers.

Meanwhile the parents have a chance to read and select books for themselves. Several bookstores mail catalogs on a regular basis:

Cover to Cover Book Store
3337 North High Street
Columbus, OH 43202

Shay Howard & Friends
11304 Sinclair Place
Northridge, CA 91326

Children, Naturally
31727 Sheridan Drive
Birmingham, MI 48009

Eeyore's Books for Children
2252 Broadway
New York, NY 10024

Pinocchio
A Bookstore for Children
826 South Aiken
Pittsburgh, PA 15232

Adventures for Kids
2760 E. Thompson Blvd.
Ventura, CA 93003

Finding Good Books

How do you find good books to buy? You can select books that are favorites from the library and that you think will remain favorites for a long time. These might include the classics many families have bought over the years: *Tom Sawyer, Heidi, The Wizard of Oz, Winnie-the-Pooh,* and numerous fairy tales.

Or you can visit a bookstore and select from its collection. Most bookstores retain buyers who have read book reviews and selected the books with the best reviews to place on sale. Small bookstores can only purchase a few of the books that are recommended, however. If you want to buy the best of the new books coming on the market, you need to look at review sources. A section on where you can find children's book reviews is included in Chapter 8: Books Too Good to Miss.

Since quantity as well as quality is important for your home collection, you need to buy both paperback and hardbound books. Garage sales are good sources of bargain books. When schools close, school library collections are sometimes put on sale. One family bought over two hundred books from a school library sale at the price of five books for a dollar! Public libraries usually have book sales each year. They are not just to rid the library of old or unpopular books; rather, these sales usually include books people have donated for the purpose of helping the library earn money. You have to look carefully to find good books in these sales, but the time is almost always worth the effort.

Grocery stores have sections devoted to children's books. Little storybooks and other inexpensive editions are tempting. Giving young children a book to look at while sitting in the seat

Youngsters enjoy reading while parents shop. It would be best, however, not to limit a child's literature to the supermarket variety.

of the shopping cart makes shopping a lot easier. Children ask to read while parents are waiting to cash checks or to check out of the store. Many of the books in grocery stores are cheaply produced versions of popular books. The illustrations are not of high quality and the versions are so condensed that they practically ruin the story. Some are simply written versions of television shows or movies. You wouldn't want to limit your child's home library to supermarket variety literature.

Book Clubs
One simple and often inexpensive source of books is a book club. There are a number of book clubs which mail a child a book a

month. Few of these, however, send high-quality children's books. Most are beginning-to-read books, or books by one author, with a very limited selection. Unfortunately, the beginning-to-read books are the very ones that a child will rapidly outgrow. For that reason, most parent-oriented book clubs are not recommended. One which does provide a variety of materials is:

D.J. Macaw Book Club
1250 Fairwood Avenue
P.O. Box 16613
Columbus, OH 43216

Schools send book club orders home with children. The classroom receives one free paperback for every five books ordered by members of the class. The discount rates are very appealing, and some of the books, cassettes, and records are of high quality. Others are gimmick books written for popular appeal.

Broadening Reading Interests

Some adults read only mystery books, only science fiction, or some other type of book. Most avid readers, however, enjoy a variety of literature. Children move through stages where they enjoy one type of book: mysteries, horse stories, dog stories, or love stories. Usually they outgrow one particular type of literature after a time. But they will not have a chance to outgrow old reading habits if they are never exposed to other kinds of books.

You can broaden your children's reading interests by looking up something on each library visit. Investigating a topic will take your children into new sections of the library where they encounter different types of books and learn how to use a variety of library services as well. Try to check out at least one nonfiction book and one record each time you visit the library.

Magazine reading is another way to broaden interests. Library visits might be scheduled to be long enough to allow for some browsing and researching as well as for finding books to check out. As children grow, their interests naturally change and expand, so don't be concerned if your children's reading habits get into a rut for a while.

Extending Books with Other Activities

After your child has read a good book, he or she needs to know how to find another one with as much appeal. Some children learn to seek out books by familiar authors. Many, however, merely flit from one book to another with no sense of direction or purpose in their reading. One technique that encourages children to acquire depth in their reading and provides linkages between what they read now and in the future is webbing. Just as a spider builds a web which branches out from a central focal point, so a reading web starts with a favorite book and branches outward. Webs can include not only other books but projects and activities as well. To make a web, brainstorm all of the possible ways of involving your child with a particular book.

For example, suppose that your child is interested in birds. A bird's nest in your yard has eggs in it. In addition to getting a telescope or binoculars with which to watch the action, write down in log form what you see. Who sits on the eggs? How many are there? What color are they? Where is the nest? How long does it take for the eggs to hatch? Are there similar nests in other places in the yard? What is the nest made of? Questions like these can be answered by observation.

Then you can look up information in bird books and reference books. *Adventuring with Books* is a wonderful resource which you can find in your library. It reviews recent books on topics of interest to children. In a recent edition, there were nineteen books about birds, including *Five Nests* by Caroline Arnold.

Another way to extend books is to web a book itself. If you've thoroughly enjoyed a book, you can think of all of the activities associated with that story which will make it more memorable and perhaps lead to further reading. For example, after reading Robert McCloskey's *Blueberries for Sal* (Viking Press, 1948), a natural follow-up activity would be to go blueberry picking and to make pies out of blueberries. Canning is another obvious follow-up activity. The book also sparks an interest in the study of berries. Which are edible, and which are not? What other kinds of berries are there, and what can be done with them?

Books should not be viewed as ends in themselves but as

windows that open thought to new ideas and lead to more investigation, study, and recreation. When your children become more than superficially interested in the books they read, their reading interests broaden and they are more likely to maintain their reading habit than if they merely jump from one book to another.

All of these strategies have a common goal: encouraging children to read for fun. Once children start thinking of reading as an adventure, they become addicted to reading.

Chapter 8

Books Too Good to Miss

"**H**ey, Jeremy! You've got to read *Half Magic*. Our teacher read it out loud and it's great!"

"Remember when they set fire to the Scarecrow of Oz? Ohhh, was I scared!"

Since children's books are the central focus of *Growing Up Reading* and since there are large numbers of books available in libraries and bookstores, it seems fitting to close with a final chapter containing book recommendations.

Book Review Sources

There are several sources of book recommendations. The Children's Book Council, 67 Irving Place, New York, NY 10003, publishes a variety of materials and sponsors Children's Book Week each year. For a small fee, you can become a lifetime member of the Children's Book Council and receive all of their promotional material. The Book Council also publishes an excellent brochure called "Choosing a Child's Book," which is free if you enclose a stamped, self-addressed envelope.

The Children's Book Council publishes a list of "Children's Choices" annually as well as selective bibliographies of social studies and science books. All of these are free if you send a self-addressed, 6 ½-by-9-inch envelope stamped for two ounces of postage. "Children's Choices" is the best short list of good, recently published books.

There are a variety of publications available that review children's literature.

Since 1980 the Cooperative Children's Book Center has read and examined over 2,000 children's books published each year. A list of their annual recommendations costs from one to two dollars and is available from:

>Friends of the CCBC, Inc.
>P.O. Box 5288
>Madison, WI 53705

Several publications review children's books and make book recommendations:

The Horn Book Magazine
31 James Avenue
Boston, MA 02116

The Kobrin Letter
732 Greer Road
Palo Alto, CA 94303

>*Parents' Choice*
>Box 185
>Waban, MA 02168

The Horn Book Magazine is the most professional of these. *Parents' Choice,* a quarterly publication, reviews movies, toys, and games as well as books. Magazines such as *Time* and *Newsweek* come out with lists of recommended books at Christmastime.

Many newspapers review books. The best-known source of these reviews is the *New York Times*, which four times a year comes out with a children's book review section. Once a year the *Times* has a list of the best books for the past year. The *Christian Science Monitor* is another national newspaper which occasionally reviews children's books. Local newspapers sporadically contain book reviews as well. If your local paper does not have such a review or a column by a librarian about new books, request that such a column be written. There may be children's literature specialists at nearby universities who might be willing to review books on a regular basis.

Libraries have a reference area in the children's department. I've found several books to be very helpful if I have a topic to look up: *The A to Zoo Subject Guide to Children's Books* by Carolyn Lima (R.R. Bowker Co., 1982), *Adventuring with Books* (NCTE, 1981), and the *Book Finder: A Guide to Children's Literature* (American Guidance Service, 1977, 1981). There are many other reference books which can help you find children's books on a variety of topics.

Librarians themselves make recommendations and they will appreciate receiving your recommendations about which books to order for the library.

Book Awards

There are many different book awards. Some are awarded for a book's illustration and design; some are awarded for the story and plot, and some are awarded because they are popular with children. Books that are rated very highly by awards committees may not be the same books which appeal to your child.

The Newbery Award is given by the American Library Association to the author of the most distinguished contribution to literature for children published in the United States during the preceding year. The award was established in 1922, so there have been many winners and runners-up.

The Caldecott Medal is also awarded by the American Library Association. It is given to the most distinguished illustration in a book for children published in the United States during the preceding year. Established in 1939, it, too, has a long list of recipients and honor books. The Newbery and Caldecott

Award-winning books are cited for their excellent literature or their outstanding illustrations.

awards have long been considered the most prestigious awards in the field of children's literature.

Each year the Children's Book Council selects the best twenty-five or thirty books from the previous year to form its Children's Book Showcase. The Showcase is a traveling exhibit which can be presented at Children's Book Fairs in local communities. A book describing the Showcase Books is published each year.

Every two years the Hans Christian Andersen Award is presented to the author and the illustrator who, in their work over a lifetime, have made important international contributions to children's literature.

Since 1979 the American Book Awards have included several awards for children's literature. Awards are given for children's fiction, children's nonfiction, and children's picture books published in this country by American authors or illustrators. A catalog of winning books can be obtained from: The American Book Awards, Association of American Publishers, One Park Avenue, New York, NY 10016.

There are also awards given for books that are popular

among children. The Georgia Book Award, for example, is given each year to the book that is the favorite of Georgia's young readers. Newly published books are distributed to teachers who encourage their students to read the books and vote for their favorites. A similar procedure is followed by the International Reading Association and the National Council of Teachers of English for their annual awards.

It is interesting (and sometimes disappointing) to read the list of books which children in a 1982 survey of over 1000 schools reported to be their favorites. Noticeably absent from the list are nonfiction books. There is only one poet mentioned (Shel Silverstein) and very few award-winning books from recent years. Many of the books on the list are currently popular realistic fiction or fantasy. Judy Blume exceeds all other authors in popularity (nine books). Beverly Cleary is second with three books on the list. There is evidence that children select favorite books by author because many of the authors are mentioned more than once (48 percent). Some authors are mentioned because of a series of books which they have written (22 percent). Only fifteen authors are mentioned because of a single book title (30 percent). A number of the books have appeared in film form on television or in movies.

Book Recommendations

Since you'll want to expose your children to a wide range of literature, recommended books are divided by subject and category. Criteria for a good book of each type are described, followed by a list of books, authors, or illustrators too good to miss. You'll be able to find these books in your local library and can order them if they aren't in your local bookstore.

Nursery Rhymes
You'll want a large Mother Goose collection. Toddlers also enjoy cardboard books and smaller volumes which contain fewer rhymes. Prereaders need the clarity of one rhyme and an accompanying picture on the page. An aspect to consider when selecting a Mother Goose collection is the percentage of rhymes which contain violence and sexism. Most Mother Goose rhymes are pure nonsense, but little children might not be aware of that.

Among the recommended nursery rhyme collections are:

Battaglia, Aurelius. *Mother Goose.* New York: Random House, 1973.

Wildsmith, Brian. *Brian Wildsmith's Mother Goose.* New York: Franklin Watts, 1964.

Wright, Blanche. *The Real Mother Goose.* Chicago: Rand McNally, 1916, 1965. (Also available in four cardboard book editions.)

Number and Concept Books

Most number and concept books have an educational orientation which makes it difficult to appreciate them as works of art. Watch for books that will enhance vocabulary. Point-and-say books need to have very clear illustrations. It is helpful if their size and color representations are as accurate as possible. A ball should not be as big as an airplane, for example.

If you want to teach alphabet letter sounds, select ABC books that use a consistent and frequently used initial sound. Alphabet books have words written out to label the pictures so that children can identify the letters in the printed word as well as the picture/word relationship.

Number and concept books should specialize in clear illustrations and well-defined ideas.

Number and counting books should have clear illustrations that are uncluttered and objects which are easily counted. *Anno's Counting Book* is an exceptionally good book, not only for its artwork but also because there are many different things to count on each page. The numeral is shown as a number, as a word, and in a stack of blocks which your child can count.

Children sometimes enjoy making their own number or concept books. You can cut out pictures from magazines to use as illustrations. Older children can draw their own illustrations.

Number and concept books are dependent upon illustrations for their success. The following illustrators are too good to miss:

Mitsumasa Anno	*Anno's Counting Book.* New York: Thomas Y. Crowell, 1977.
	Anno's Counting House. New York: Philomel Books, 1982.
Molly Bang	*Ten, Nine, Eight.* New York: Greenwillow, 1983.
Byron Barton	*Building a House.* New York: Greenwillow, 1981.
	Wheels. New York: Thomas Y. Crowell, 1979.
Eric Carle	*The Very Hungry Caterpillar.* Collins-World, 1969, 1972.
	The Honeybee and the Robber. New York: Philomel Books (Putnam), 1981.
Donald Crews	*Truck.* New York: Greenwillow Books, 1980.
	Freight Train. New York: Greenwillow Books, 1978.
Gyo Fujikawa	*Let's Play.* New York: Grosset & Dunlap, 1975.

Tana Hoban	*Round and Round and Round.* New York: Greenwillow, 1983. *Take Another Look.* New York: Greenwillow, 1981.
Pat Hutchins	*Rosie's Walk.* New York: Macmillan, 1968. *Clocks and More Clocks.* New York: Macmillan, 1970.
Virginia Jensen	*Catching.* New York: Philomel, 1983.
Stan Mack	*10 Bears in My Bed.* New York: Pantheon, 1974.
Bruno Munari	*Bruno Munari's Zoo.* New York: Putnam, 1963.
Ken Robbins	*Tools.* New York: Four Winds Press, 1983.
Brian Wildsmith	*Brian Wildsmith's 1,2,3.* New York: Franklin Watts, 1965. *What the Moon Saw.* London: Oxford University Press, 1978.

Wordless Picture Books

Wordless picture books depend upon the pictures to tell the story or present the concept in the book. The picture stories in most wordless books are so sophisticated that, even though there are no words, they are appropriate for older children.

Wordless picture books help young children develop visual perception, remember details (in this case details within pictures), and anticipate outcomes of sequential tales. Children can tell and tape-record stories to go with wordless picture books.

Goodall, John. *Paddy's New Hat.* New York: Atheneum, 1980.
——. *The Surprise Picnic.* New York: Atheneum, 1977.

Wordless picture books rely on clever illustrations and a child's imagination.

Mayer, Mercer. *A Boy, a Frog, and a Dog* (series). New York: Dial Press, 1967.

Young, Ed. *Up A Tree*. New York: Harper & Row, 1983.

Folktales and fairy tales have been published in a variety of well-written, attractive versions.

Folktales and Fairy Tales

Since folktales and fairy tales have been handed down orally through the years, there are many different written versions of

Growing Up Reading 173

them. These stories are ideal to read aloud with children as they follow the illustrations, so it is important that the illustrations are entertaining.

The following authors and illustrators are especially successful at presenting folk literature in picture book format:

Marcia Brown	*Cinderella.* (C. Perrault), New York: Charles Scribner's Sons, 1953. *Once a Mouse.* New York: Charles Scribner's Sons, 1961. *Stone Soup.* New York: Charles Scribner's Sons, 1942.
Tomie De Paola	*The Clown of God.* New York: Harcourt Brace Jovanovich, 1978. *The Legend of the Bluebonnet: an Old Tale of Texas.* New York: G.P. Putnam's Sons, 1983. *The Prince of the Dolomites.* New York: Harcourt Brace Jovanovich, 1980.
Paul Galdone	*The Little Red Hen.* Boston: Houghton Mifflin, 1973. New York: Scholastic, 1975. *The Three Bears.* New York: Scholastic, 1973. *The Three Billy Goats Gruff.* Boston: Houghton Mifflin, 1981. *The Magic Porridge Pot.* Boston: Houghton Mifflin, 1976.
Mirra Ginsburg	*Mushroom in the Rain.* Translated by V. Suteyev. Illustrated by Jose Aruego and Adriane Dewey. New York: Macmillan, 1974. *Where Does the Sun Go at Night?* Illustrated by Jose Aruego and Adriane Dewey. Boston: Greenwillow Books, 1981.

Paul Goble	*The Girl Who Loved Wild Horses.* New York: Bradbury Press, 1978. *Star Boy.* New York: Bradbury Press, 1983.
Nonny Hogrogian	*One Fine Day.* New York: Macmillan, 1971. *The Devil with the Three Golden Hairs.* New York: Alfred A. Knopf, 1983.
Trina Schart Hyman	*Little Red Riding Hood.* New York: Holiday House, 1983. *The Sleeping Beauty* (Grimm). Boston: Little, Brown, 1977.
Susan Jeffers	*Hansel and Gretel* (Grimm). New York: Dial Press, 1980. *Thumbelina* (Andersen). New York: Dial Press, 1979.
Arlene Mosel	*Tikki Tikki Tembo.* Illustrated by Blair Lent. Holt, Rinehart & Winston, 1968. *The Funny Little Woman.* Illustrated by Blair Lent. E.P. Dutton, 1972.
Lisbeth Zwerger	*Little Red Cap* (Grimm). Translated by Elizabeth Crawford. New York: William Morrow, 1983.

Picture Story Books
Notice the quality of picture book illustrations as well as the quality of the story. Good picture books have stories which could stand on their own without illustration, yet the pictures are works of art. Illustrators use many different types of paint, crayons, pencils, collage techniques, prints, photographs, and combinations of these to create their artwork. You and your child might seek out books using one particular medium, then try your skill at that art medium. Books expose children to

Good picture story books are noted for their excellent illustrations and their high-interest stories.

quality art. How important it becomes, then, to find picture books with the best art.

These authors and illustrators have produced books with outstanding illustrations, a strong story line, and appeal to children.

Martha Alexander	*I Sure Am Glad to See You, Black Bear.* New York: Dial Press, 1976. *Maggie's Moon.* New York: Dial Press, 1982.
Virginia Lee Burton	*Mike Mulligan and His Steam Shovel* Boston: Houghton Mifflin, 1939. *The Little House.* Boston: Houghton Mifflin, 1942.
Barbara Cooney	*Miss Rumphius.* New York: Viking Press, 1982.
Janina Domanska	*I Saw a Ship A-Sailing.* New York: Greenwillow, 1980. *King Krakus and the Dragon.* New York: Greenwillow, 1979.

Lisa Ernst	*Sam Johnson and the Blue Ribbon Quilt.* New York: Lothrop, 1983.
Marie Hall Ets	*Gilberto and the Wind.* New York: Viking, 1963. *Just Me.* New York: Viking, 1965.
Marjorie Flack	*Ask Mister Bear.* New York: Macmillan, 1932, 1958. *Angus and the Cat.* Garden City, N. Y.: Doubleday, 1931. *The Story about Ping.* New York: Viking, 1933.
Don Freeman	*Bearymore.* New York: Viking, 1976. *Corduroy.* New York: Viking, 1968. *Dandelion.* New York: Viking, 1964. *Flash the Dash.* Chicago: Children's Press, 1973.
Wilson Gage	*Cully Cully and the Bear.* New York: Greenwillow, 1983.
Russell Hoban	*Bedtime for Frances.* New York: Harper & Row, 1960. *Best Friends for Frances.* New York: Harper & Row, 1969.
Ezra Jack Keats	*Peter's Chair.* New York: Harper & Row, 1967. *The Snowy Day.* New York: Viking Press, 1962. *The Trip.* New York: Greenwillow, 1978. *Whistle for Willie.* New York: Viking, 1964.

Steven Kellogg	*The Island of the Skog.* New York: Dial Press, 1973. *Pinkerton, Behave!* New York: Dial Press, 1979.
Leo Lionni	*Frederick.* New York: Pantheon, 1967. *Inch by Inch.* New York: Astor, 1960. *Alexander and the Wind-Up Mouse.* New York: Pantheon, 1969.
James Marshall	*George and Martha Back in Town.* New York: Houghton Mifflin, 1984.
Robert McCloskey	*Make Way for Ducklings.* New York: Viking, 1941. *One Morning in Maine.* New York: Viking, 1952. *Blueberries for Sal.* New York: Viking, 1948.
Mercer Mayer	*Liza Lou and the Yeller Belly Swamp.* New York: Parents' Magazine Press, 1976. *There's a Nightmare in My Closet.* New York: Dial Press, 1968.
Ellen Raskin	*Nothing Ever Happens on My Block.* New York: Atheneum, 1966. *Spectacles.* New York: Atheneum, 1968.
Maurice Sendak	*In the Night Kitchen.* New York: Harper & Row, 1970. *Where the Wild Things Are.* New York: Harper & Row, 1963.

Esphyr Slopbodkina	*Caps for Sale.* Reading, Mass.: Addison-Wesley, 1947.
William Steig	*The Amazing Bone.* New York: Farrar, Straus & Giroux, 1976. *Tiffky Doofky.* New York: Farrar, Straus & Giroux, 1978.
Brinton Turkle	*The Adventures of Obadiah.* New York: Viking, 1972.
Chris Van Allsburg	*The Wreck of the Zephyr.* Boston: Houghton Mifflin, 1983.
Judith Viorst	*Alexander and the Terrible, Horrible, No Good, Very Bad Day.* Illustrated by Ray Cruz. New York: Atheneum, 1972.
Bernard Waber	*Ira Sleeps Over.* Boston: Houghton Mifflin, 1972. *Lyle, Lyle, Crocodile.* Boston: Houghton Mifflin, 1965.
Taro Yashima	*Crow Boy.* New York: Viking, 1955. *Umbrella.* New York: Viking, 1958.
Charlotte Zolotow	*William's Doll.* Illustrated by William Pène du Bois. New York: Harper & Row, 1972. *My Grandson, Lew.* Illustrated by William Pène du Bois. New York: Harper & Row, 1974.

Poetry

Children usually prefer humorous poems with strong rhythm and rhyme over unrhymed poetry, such as haiku and cinquain. You might take a poetry book out of the library each week along with your fiction books. Your family can develop their own collection of favorite poems.

There are many fine collections of poetry that parents will enjoy sharing with their children.

There are collections of short poems and whole stories written in rhyme. A good collection is the *Random House Book of Poetry for Children* (Edited by Jack Prelutsky. Illustrated by Arnold Lobel. 1983).

Each year, the National Council of Teachers of English honors a living American poet in recognition of his or her life's work. Winners have included:

David McCord   *Speak Up: More Rhymes of the Never Was and Always Is.* Illustrated by Marc Simont. Boston: Little, Brown, 1980.
One At a Time: Collected Poems for the Young. Illustrated by Henry B. Kane. Boston: Little, Brown, 1977.

Aileen Fisher	*I Stood Upon a Mountain.* Illustrated by Blair Lent. New York: Thomas Y. Crowell, 1979. *Out in the Dark and Daylight.* Illustrated by Gail Owens. New York: Harper & Row, 1980.
Karla Kuskin	*Any Me I Want to Be.* New York: Harper & Row, 1972. *Dogs and Dragons, Trees and Dreams.* New York: Harper & Row, 1980.
Myra Cohn Livingston	*A Lollygag of Limericks.* Illustrated by Joseph Low. New York: Atheneum New York: 1978. *O Sliver of Liver.* Illustrated by Iris Van Rynbach. New York: Atheneum, 1979.
Eve Merriam	*It Doesn't Always Have to Rhyme.* Illustrated by Malcolm Spooner. New York: Atheneum, 1964. *There Is No Rhyme for Silver.* Illustrated by Joseph Schindelman. New York: Atheneum, 1962.
John Ciardi	*Fast and Slow.* Illustrated by Becky Gaver. Boston: Houghton Mifflin, 1975. *Someone Could Win a Polar Bear.* Illustrated by Edward Gorey. Philadelphia: Lippincott, 1970.

Other good poetry books include:

Mary Ann Hoberman	*Bugs.* Illustrated by Victoria Chess. New York: Viking, 1976.

Lee Bennett Hopkins	*Surprises.* New York: Harper & Row, 1984. *Morning, Noon, & Nighttime, Too.* Illustrated by Nancy Hannans. New York: Harper & Row, 1980.
Susan Jeffers	*Hiawatha* (Henry Wadsworth Longfellow). New York: E.P. Dutton, 1983.
Hilary Knight	*The Owl and the Pussy-Cat* (Edward Lear). New York: Macmillan, 1983.
Nancy Larrick	*Piping Down the Valleys Wild.* New York: Dell, 1970. *On City Streets.* Illustrated by David Sagarin. New York: M. Evans, 1968.
Jean Marzollo	*Close Your Eyes.* Illustrated by Susan Jeffers. New York: Dial Press, 1978.
Charles Mikolaycak	*The Highwayman* (Alfred Noyes). New York: Lothrop, Lee & Shepard, 1983. *Bring Me All of Your Dreams.* Photos by Larry Mulvehill. New York: M. Evans, 1980.
Nancy Patz	*Moses Supposes His Toeses are Roses and 7 Other Silly Old Rhymes.* New York: Harcourt Brace Jovanovich, 1983.
Shel Silverstein	*A Light in the Attic.* New York: Harper & Row, 1981. *Where the Sidewalk Ends.* New York: Harper & Row, 1974.

Diane Stanley   *Little Orphant Annie* (James
                          Whitcomb Riley). New York:
                          Putnam, 1983.

Robert L. Stevenson   *A Child's Garden of Verses.* Illustrated
                          by Ruth Sanderson. New York:
                          Platt & Munk, 1977.

Clyde Watson   *Father Fox's Pennyrhymes.* New York:
                          Harper & Row, 1971; Scholastic,
                          1975.
                          Father Fox's Feast of Songs Applebet.
                          New York: Farrar, Straus &
                          Giroux, 1982.

Fantasy and science fiction are very popular among young readers.

Fantasy and Science Fiction
Fantasy is one of the most popular forms of fiction among children. Many fantasy books have animals serving as main characters. Both fantasy and science fiction are deceptively simple types of literature. Underlying the fantasy has to be the appearance of realism. Unless the story appears plausible,

Growing Up Reading   183

children dismiss it as unbelievable and uninteresting. In science fiction scientific truths are observed with only one element of fiction. Writers must stay within these boundaries when writing fanciful stories.

There are two elements of fantasy that are the focus of most stories. Either the story is about an imaginary character—a toy, an animal, or a tiny person—or the story departs from the real world with a series of curious occurrences—people fly, travel through time, or perform superhuman tasks.

Alexander, Lloyd. *The High King*. New York: Holt, Rinehart and Winston, 1968.
———. *The Kestrel*. New York: E.P. Dutton, 1982.
Babbitt, Natalie. *The Devil's Storybook*. New York: Farrar, Straus & Giroux, 1974.
———. *Tuck Everlasting*. New York: Farrar, Straus & Giroux, 1975.
Christopher, John. *Fireball*. New York: E.P. Dutton, 1981.
Cooper, Susan. *The Dark Is Rising*. New York: Atheneum, 1973.
———. *Silver on the Tree*. New York: Atheneum, 1977.
Dahl, Roald. *The BFG*. New York: Farrar, Straus & Giroux, 1982.
———. *Charlie and the Chocolate Factory*. New York: Knopf, 1964.
———. *James and the Giant Peach*. New York: Knopf, 1961.
Eager, Edward. *Half Magic*. Illustrated by N. M. Bodecker. New York: Harcourt Brace, 1954.
———. *Seven Day Magic*. Illustrated by N. M. Bodecker. New York: Harcourt Brace, 1962.
Grahame, Kenneth. *The Wind in the Willows*. Illustrated by Ernest H. Shepard. New York: Charles Scribner's Sons, 1953. Many editions.
Hamilton, Virginia. *The Gathering*. New York: Greenwillow, 1981.
———. *Jahdu*. Illustrated by Jerry Pinkney. New York: Greenwillow, 1980.
Juster, Norton. *The Phantom Tollbooth*. Illustrated by Jules Feiffer. New York: Random House, 1961.
Kipling, Rudyard. *Just-So Stories*. New York: Doubleday, Page & Co., 1902.
Lawson, Robert. *Rabbit Hill*. New York: Viking, 1944.

Lewis, C. S. *The Lion, the Witch and the Wardrobe.* Illustrated by Pauline Baynes. New York: Macmillan, 1961.

L'Engle, Madeleine. *A Wrinkle in Time.* New York: Farrar, Straus & Giroux, 1962.

Milne, A. A. *Winnie-the-Pooh.* New York: E.P. Dutton, 1926.

Norton, Mary. *The Borrowers.* New York: Harcourt, 1953.

O'Brien, Robert. *Mrs. Frisby and the Rats of NIMH.* New York: Atheneum, 1971.

Potter, Beatrix. *The Tale of Peter Rabbit* (and others). London: Warne, various dates.

Steig, William. *Abel's Island.* New York: Farrar, Straus & Giroux, 1972.

Tolkien, J.R.R. *The Hobbit.* Boston: Houghton Mifflin, 1938.

Travers, P. L. *Mary Poppins.* New York: Harcourt Brace Jovanovich, 1934, 1981.

White, E.B. *Charlotte's Web.* Illustrated by Garth Williams. New York: Harper & Row, 1952.

———. *Stuart Little.* Illustrated by Garth Williams. New York: Harper & Row, 1973.

General Fiction

There are many types of fiction for children. A good work of fiction is realistic enough for the reader to believe that it could have taken place. Good realistic fiction is written in a fresh, but not faddish, style. Even if the content becomes dated it lasts because it is well-written. Some authors of realistic fiction try to preach unobtrusively in their stories, but good realistic fiction is not overly instructional.

Today, realistic fiction covers topics not mentioned a few years ago in children's books—death, divorce, sex, and religion—topics some parents may not want their children to read until they are mature enough to handle them. Most younger children shun books they do not understand anyway. You may find that monitoring your children's reading provides opportunities for good open-ended discussions that would not have occurred if your children had not been reading books on these topics.

Some realistic books are so popular that children read them over and over again. Horse stories and dog stories are examples.

Good fiction should seem so real that the reader believes it could really happen.

Some children go through a period where they read nothing but mystery stories or sports stories. Humorous fiction stories are also enjoyed by almost all children.

If your children like a particular type of fiction, they should be encouraged to look up more books on that topic in the subject index of the card catalog in the library. There are many lists of good books in each area of fiction, particularly on controversial topics. Generally, these books provide material for children to think about and discuss with a sensitive adult.

Recommending fiction is difficult since each person's tastes vary and some books are more appropriate for older rather than younger children. The following list of books and authors provides a core group of titles which children will not want to miss:

Brittain, Bill. *Wish Giver.* New York: Harper, 1983.

Byars, Betsy. *Good-bye, Chicken Little.* New York: Harper & Row, 1979.

———. *The Night Swimmers.* Illustrated by Troy Howell. New York: Delacorte, 1980.

———. *The Pinballs.* New York: Harper & Row, 1977.

———. *Summer of the Swans.* Illustrated by Ted CoConis. New York: Viking Press, 1970.

Cleary, Beverly. *Dear Mr. Henshaw.* New York: Morrow, 1983.
——. *Ralph S. Mouse* (series). New York: Morrow, 1982.
——. *Ramona Forever.* New York: Morrow, 1984.
Corbett, Scott. *The Donkey Planet.* Illustrated by Troy Howell. New York: E.P. Dutton, 1979.
——. *The Turnabout Trick.* Illustrated by Paul Galdone. Boston: Little, Brown, 1967.
Cunningham, Julia. *Dorp Dead.* Illustrated by James Spanfeller. New York: Pantheon, 1965.
Fitzhugh, Louise. *Harriet the Spy.* New York: Harper, 1964.
Fox, Paula. *A Girl Called Al.* Illustrated by Byron Barton. New York: Viking, 1969.
——. *Maurice's Room.* Illustrated by Ingrid Fetz. New York: Macmillan 1966.
George, Jean Craighead. *Talking Earth.* New York: Harper & Row, 1983.
Greene, Constance. *I and Sproggy.* Illustrated by Emily McCully. New York: Viking, 1978.
——. *Your Old Pal.* New York: Viking, 1979.
Hahn, Mary. *Daphne's Book.* New York: Clarion, 1983.
Hamilton, Virginia. *The House of Dies Drear.* Illustrated by Eros Keith. New York: Macmillan, 1968.
——. *Zeely.* New York: Macmillan, 1967.
Haywood, Carolyn. *"B" Is for Betsy* (series). New York: Harcourt Brace Jovanovich, 1939; Voyager, 1968.
——. *Eddie and the Fire Engine* (series). New York: Morrow, 1949.
Henry, Marguerite. *Misty of Chincoteague.* Chicago: Rand McNally, 1947.
——. *Stormy, Misty's Foal.* Illustrated by Wesley Dennis. Chicago: Rand McNally, 1963.
Konigsburg, E. L. *From the Mixed-Up Files of Mrs. Basil E. Frankweiler.* New York: Atheneum, 1967.
Lasky, Kathryn. *Night Journey.* New York: Warne, 1981.
McCloskey, Robert. *Homer Price.* New York: Viking, 1943
Paterson, Katherine. *Bridge to Terabithia.* New York: Thomas Y. Crowell, 1977.
——. *The Great Gilly Hopkins.* New York: Thomas Y. Crowell, 1978.

Robertson, Keith. *Henry Reed Inc.* Illustrated by Robert McCloskey. New York: Viking, 1958.

Shreve, Susan. *Flunking of Joshua T. Bates.* New York: Knopf, 1984.

Smith, Doris. *Kelly's Creek.* Illustrated by Alan Tiegreen. New York: Thomas Y. Crowell, 1975.

———. *A Taste of Blackberries.* Illustrated by Charles Robinson. Thomas Y. Crowell, 1973.

Wright, Betty Ren. *Dollhouse Murders.* New York: Holiday, 1983.

If children enjoy reading one book from a series, they'll usually seek out more from that series.

Series Books

Several authors are well-known not for one excellent book but for a series. Series books are perfect for enticing children (especially reluctant readers) to read more. Children who enjoy one book in a series return to seek out others. Series books vary in difficulty from easy-to-read series to challenging historical and realistic fiction. The series listed below are among the most popular. One book from each series is listed. All of these books are available as paperbacks.

Bemelmans, Ludwig. *Madeline.* New York: Viking, 1939, 1951.

Bond, Michael. *Paddington on Top.* Illustrated by Peggy Fortnum. Boston: Houghton Mifflin, 1975.

Boston, L.M. *The Treasure of Green Knowe.* Illustrated by Peter Boston. New York: Harcourt Brace Jovanovich, 1958.

Calhoun, Mary. *Katie John.* New York: Harper & Row, 1960.

Duvoisin, Roger. *Petunia.* New York: Knopf, 1950.

Fleishman, Sid. *McBroom the Rainmaker.* New York: Grosset & Dunlap, 1973.

Hildick, E.W. *McGurk Gets Good and Bad.* New York: Macmillan, 1982.

Lindgren, Astrid. *Pippi Goes on Board* (Pippi Longstocking series). Translated by Florence Lamborn. Illustrated by Louis Glanzman. New York: Viking, 1957.

MacGregor, Ellen. *Miss Pickerell Goes to Mars.* New York: McGraw-Hill, 1951.

McInerney, Judith. *Judge Benjamin: Super Dog.* New York: Holiday House, 1982.

Norton, Mary. *The Borrowers.* New York: Harcourt Brace, 1953.

Quackenbush, Robert. *Piet Potter to the Rescue: Book I.* New York: McGraw, 1981.

Rey, H.A. *Curious George.* Boston: Houghton Mifflin, 1941.

Sobol, Donald. *Encyclopedia Brown and the Case of the Dead Eagles.* Illustrated by Leonard Shorthall, Camden, N.J.: Nelson, 1975.

Tanner, Mary. *The Wizard Children of Finn.* New York: Knopf, 1981.

Taylor, Sydney. *Ella of All-of-a-Kind.* Illustrated by Gail Owens. New York: E.P. Dutton, 1978.

Biography and Historical Fiction

Good historical fiction is accurate but not heavy in fact. The story is entertaining. Stereotypes are avoided while, at the same time, the story is factual. Readers feel as though they are transplanted to other times and cultures. Stories are entertaining and never become dated because they contain universal qualities. Most works of historical fiction have been researched in depth by their authors. Younger readers enjoy historical fiction in the form of picture books. Several outstanding examples include: the Obadiah books by Brinton Turkle, about a Quaker family on Nantucket Island; *The Ox-Cart Man* by Donald Hall, about a family trading at Portsmouth Harbor in colonial times; and the winner of the Caldecott Award, *The Glorious Flight.*

Good historical fiction makes the reader feel he has been transported into another time.

More picture books of this quality are needed.

Aliki. *A Medieval Feast.* New York: Thomas Y. Crowell, 1983.

Hall, Donald. *The Ox-Cart Man.* Illustrated by Barbara Cooney. New York: Viking, 1979.

Provensen, Alice and Martin. *The Glorious Flight across the Channel with Louis Bleriot.* New York: Viking, 1983.

Turkle, Brinton. *The Adventures of Obadiah.* New York: Viking, 1972.

    Examples of historical fiction for older children include:

Blos, Joan. *A Gathering of Days: A New England Girl's Journal, 1930-32.* New York: Charles Scribner's Sons, 1979.

Collier, James Lincoln and Christopher Collier. *My Brother Sam Is Dead.* New York: Four Winds, 1974.

Dalgliesh, Alice. *The Courage of Sarah Noble.* Illustrated by Leonard Weisgard. New York: Charles Scribner's Sons, 1954.

Forbes, Esther. *Johnny Tremain.* Illustrated by Lynd Ward. Boston: Houghton Mifflin, 1943.

Guach, Patricia Lee. *This Time, Tempe Wicke?* Illustrated by Margot Tomes. New York: Coward, McCann, 1974.

Greene, Bett. *The Summer of My German Soldier.* New York: Dial, 1973.

Monjo, F. N. *The Drinking Gourd.* Illustrated by Fred Brenner. New York: Harper & Row, 1970.

O'Dell, Scott. *Sarah Bishop.* Boston: Houghton Mifflin, 1980.
——. *Sing Down the Moon.* Boston: Houghton Mifflin, 1970.
Paterson, Katherine. *The Master Puppeteer.* Illustrated by Haru Wells. New York: Thomas Y. Crowell, 1975.
Steele, William O. *The Magic Amulet.* New York: Harcourt Brace Jovanovich, 1979.
——. *The Perilous Road.* Illustrated by Paul Galdone. New York: Harcourt, 1958.
Wilder, Laura Ingalls. *Little House on the Prairie.* New York: Harper & Row, various dates.

Biographies can be nonfiction or fictionalized, but they should be accurate and entertaining. Like historical fiction, biography tends to focus upon the famous and sensational events rather than the common people and ordinary times. In many cases individuals who lived in the past are made to look like superheroes in children's biographies. Unfortunately, there are few good biographies for children. Jean Fritz is the best-known writer of biography for children. Her books take an incident from a person's background and report it entertainingly in short books. An example is *And Then What Happened, Paul Revere?*

Other biographies include:

Blackburn, Joyce. *James Edward Oglethorpe.* New York: Dodd, 1983.
Brandenburg, Alik. *The Many Lives of Benjamin Franklin.* Englewood Cliffs, N.J.: Prentice-Hall, 1977.
Buchard, Marshall. *Sports Hero: Pete Rose.* New York: Putnam, 1976.
Dank, Milton. *Albert Einstein.* New York: Franklin Watts, 1983.
Fritz, Jean. *Can't You Make Them Behave, King George?* Illustrated by Tomie De Paola. New York: Coward, McCann, 1977.
——. *Stonewall.* Illustrated by Stephen Gammell. New York: G. P. Putnam's, 1979.
Hamilton, Virginia. *Paul Robeson, The Life and Times of a Free Black Man.* New York: Harper & Row, 1974.
Harris, Jacqueline. *Martin Luther King, Jr..* New York: Franklin Watts, 1983.
Kytle, Calvin. *Gandhi: Soldier of Nonviolence.* Seven Locks Press, 1983.

Lasker, David. *The Boy Who Loved Music.* New York: Viking, 1979.
Lawson, Robert. *Ben and Me.* Boston: Little, Brown, 1939, 1951.
Lepsky, Ibi. *Leonardo DaVinci.* New York: Barrons, 1984.
O'Connor, Karen. *Sally Ride and the New Astronauts.* New York: Franklin Watts, 1983.
Quackenbush, Robert. *Quick, Annie, Give Me a Catchy Line! A Story of Samuel F. B. Morse.* Englewood Cliffs, N.J.: Prentice Hall, 1983.
Yates, Elizabeth. *Amos Fortune, Free Man.* New York: E.P. Dutton, 1956.

General Nonfiction
There are other nonfiction children's books on practically any topic. The good ones have clear, realistic illustrations (often photographs) and are interestingly written. Some recent nonfiction books of high quality include:
Anno, Masaichiro, and Mitsumasa Anno. *Anno's Mysterious Multiplying Jar.* New York: Philomel, 1983.
Branley, Franklyn. *Halley: Comet, 1986.* New York: Lodestar/Dutton, 1983.
Burns, Marilyn. *Math for Smarty Pants.* Boston: Little, Brown, 1982.
Cole, Joanna. *How You Were Born.* New York: William Morrow, 1984.
Pringle, Laurence. *Being a Plant.* New York: Thomas Y. Crowell, 1983.
Simon, Seymour. *The Optical Illusion Book.* New York: Four Winds, 1976.
Yabuchi, Marayuki. *Animals Sleeping.* New York: Philomel, 1981. Franklin Watts Science World Series, 1983. Living Here Series, New York: Bookwright, 1984.

There are many wonderful children's books available in libraries and book stores. The preceding lists are in no way intended to be all-inclusive. Because children's experiences and interests vary widely, it is impossible to recommend precisely for an individual books on a condensed list. If you start with books on this list, however, they will undoubtedly lead you to other equally fascinating children's books.

Conclusion

In a book containing as many ideas as this one, it seems important to step back at the end and to draw some conclusions about what has been said. None of the individual ideas presented in this book in and of themselves is going to drastically improve a child's progress in reading. Rather, it is the overall message of the book that is going to make a difference. The book's message can be summarized with the following points:
- you are the most important teacher that your child will ever have;
- much of the teaching you do is simply responding to your child's curiosity;
- much of the teaching you do is very informal and can hardly be called "teaching" at all;
- this informal instruction is wonderfully enjoyable to the entire family—the benefits of reading aloud and encouraging children to develop as readers are equally satisfying for parents;
- even after children are in school you need to encourage, enrich, and expand your child's opportunities for reading.

You can be assured that your positive attitudes about your child's progress in reading will reap huge dividends in his or her enthusiasm for reading. Skill in reading develops from this enthusiasm, which drives children to do a lot of reading. Practice makes perfect. Children are not necessarily avid readers just because they know how to read well; rather, children who are avid readers develop advanced reading skills, especially if their parents are involved in their reading development.

Out of all of the specific ideas presented in this book, which are the most crucial to remember?
- Immerse your child in print by reading aloud and by pointing out writing in the environment.
- Write with your child and provide materials and opportunities for independent writing.
- Talk with your child about what he or she is reading.

- Link reading to the activities and interests of the family.
- Provide quality time for reading on a daily basis.
- Provide a variety of reading materials of high interest.
- Observe how your child is progressing in reading and be responsive to his or her needs.
- Don't correct your child's reading errors or criticize his selection of books.

Families who enthusiastically embrace reading as a family activity find that the joys of reading are immeasurable. There is no greater pleasure than watching children who grow up reading.

Appendix

Publishers and Their Addresses

Abelard-Schuman
257 Park Avenue
New York, NY 10010

Abingdon Press
201 Eighth Avenue South
Nashville, TN 37202

Acropolis Books, Ltd.
2400 17th Street, NW
Washington, DC 20009

Addison-Wesley Publishing
  Co., Inc.
Jacob Way
Reading, MA 01867

Allyn & Bacon Inc.
7 Wells Avenue
Newton, MA 02159

Ariel (Farrar)
19 Union Square
New York, NY 10003

Astor Honor
48 East 43rd Street
New York, NY 10017

Atheneum Publishers
597 Fifth Avenue
New York, NY 10017

The Atlantic Monthly Press
8 Arlington Street
Boston, MA 02116

Avon Books
1790 Broadway
New York, NY 10019

Ballantine Books, Inc.
201 E. 50th Street
New York, NY 10022

Bantam Books
666 Fifth Avenue
New York, NY 10103

Barnes & Noble Books
10 E. 53rd Street
New York, NY 10022

Barron's Educational Series
  Inc.
113 Crossways Park Drive
Woodbury, NY 11797

Beacon Press
25 Beacon Street
Boston, MA 02108

Bobbs-Merrill
Box 558
4300 West 62nd Street
Indianapolis, IN 46206

R.R. Bowker and Co.
205 East 42nd Street
New York, NY 10017

Bowmar
Box 3623
Glendale, CA 91201

Bradbury Press, Inc.
2 Overhill Road
Scarsdale, NY 10583

William C. Brown Co.,
    Publishers
2460 Kerper Boulevard
Dubuque, IA 52001

Carolrhoda Books
241 First Avenue North
Minneapolis, MN 55401

Children's Book Council, Inc.
67 Irving Place
New York, NY 10003

Children's Press
1224 West Van Buren Street
Chicago, IL 60607

Clarion Books
52 Vanderbilt Avenue
New York, NY 10017

William Collins Publishers,
    Inc.
200 Madison Avenue
New York, NY 10016

Council on Interracial Books
    for Children
1841 Broadway
New York, NY 10023

Coward, McCann &
    Geoghegan, Inc.
200 Madison Avenue
New York, NY 10016

Crowell Junior Books
(Harper Junior Books Group)
10 East 53rd Street
New York, NY 10022

Creative Education Inc.
Box 227
123 South Broad Street
Mankato, MN 56001

Crown Publishers, Inc.
One Park Avenue
New York, NY 10016

John Day
(Harper & Row, Inc.)
10 East 53rd Street
New York, NY 10022

Delacorte Press
1 Dag Hammarskjold Plaza
245 East 47th Street
New York, NY 10017

Dell Publishing Co., Inc.
1 Dag Hammarskjold Plaza
245 East 47th Street
New York, NY 10017

Design Enterprises of San Francisco
Box 14695
San Francisco, CA 94114

The Dial Books for Young Readers
(E.P. Dutton, Inc.)
2 Park Avenue
New York, NY 10016

Dodd, Mead & Co., Inc.
79 Madison Avenue
New York, NY 10016

Doubleday & Co., Inc.
245 Park Avenue
New York, NY 10167

Dover Publications, Inc.
180 Varick Street
New York, NY 10014

E.P. Dutton
2 Park Avenue
New York, NY 10016

Elsevier/Nelson Books
2 Park Avenue
New York, NY 10016

M. Evans & Co., Inc.
216 East 49th Street
New York, NY 10017

Faber & Faber, Inc.
39 Thompson Street
Winchester, MA 01890

Farrar, Straus & Giroux, Inc.
19 Union Square West
New York, NY 10003

The Feminist Press
Box 334
Old Westbury, NY 11568

Follett Publishing Co.
1010 West Washington Boulevard
Chicago, IL 60607

Four Winds Press
730 Broadway
New York, NY 10003

Garrard Publishing
1607 North Market Street
Champaign, IL 61820

Golden Press (Western Publishing)
1220 Mound Avenue
Racine, WI 53404

Greenwillow Books
(A Division of William
   Morrow & Co.)
105 Madison Avenue
New York, NY 10016

Grosset & Dunlap, Inc.
51 Madison Avenue
New York, NY 10010

G. K. Hall & Co.
70 Lincoln Street
Boston, MA 02111

Harcourt Brace Jovanovich,
   Inc.
1250 Sixth Avenue
San Diego, CA 92101

Harper & Row, Publishers,
   Inc.
10 East 53rd Street
New York, NY 10022

Harvey House, Publishers
20 Waterside Plaza
New York, NY 10010

Hastings House Publishers,
   Inc.
10 East 40th Street
New York, NY 10016

Heinemann Educational
   Books Inc.
70 Court Street
Portsmouth, NH 03801

Holiday House
18 East 53rd Street
New York, NY 10022

Holt, Rinehart & Winston
521 Fifth Avenue
6th Floor
New York, NY 10175

Houghton Mifflin Co.
2 Park Street
Boston, MA 02108

Alfred A. Knopf, Inc.
201 East 50th Street
New York, NY 10022

Larousse & Co., Inc.
572 Fifth Avenue
New York, NY 10036

Lerner Publications
241 First Avenue North
Minneapolis, MN 55401

Lippincott Junior Books
(Harper Junior Books Group)
10 East 53rd Street
New York, NY 10022

Little, Brown & Co.
34 Beacon Street
Boston, MA 02106

Lothrop, Lee & Shepard Co.
105 Madison Avenue
New York, NY 10016

McGraw-Hill Book Co.
1221 Avenue of the Americas
New York, NY 10020

David McKay
750 Third Avenue
New York, NY 10017

Macmillan Publishing Co., Inc.
866 Third Avenue
New York, NY 10022

Charles E. Merrill Pub. Co.
1300 Alum Creek Drive
Columbus, OH 43216

Julian Messner
(Simon & Schuster, Inc.)
1230 Avenue of the Americas
New York, NY 10020

Methuen, Inc.
733 Third Avenue
New York, NY 10017

William Morrow & Co., Inc.
105 Madison Avenue
New York, NY 10016

The New American Library, Inc.
1633 Broadway
New York, NY 10019

Oxford University Press
200 Madison Avenue
New York, NY 10016

Pantheon Books
201 East 50th Street
New York, NY 10022

Parents Magazine Press
685 Third Avenue
New York, NY 10017

Penguin Books, Inc.
40 West 23rd Street
New York, NY 10010

Philomel Books
51 Madison Avenue
New York, NY 10010

Platt & Munk
(Grosset & Dunlap)
51 Madison Avenue
New York, NY 10010

Plays, Inc.
8 Arlington Street
Boston, MA 02116

Pocket Books
1230 Avenue of the Americas
New York, NY 10020

Prentice-Hall, Inc.
Englewood Cliffs, NJ 07632

G. P. Putnam's Sons
51 Madison Avenue
New York, NY 10010

Harlin Quist Books
192 East 75th Street
New York, NY 10021

Rand McNally & Co.
P.O. Box 7600
Chicago, IL 60680

Random House
201 East 50th Street
New York, NY 10022

Schocken Books, Inc.
200 Madison Avenue
New York, NY 10016

Scholastic Inc.
730 Broadway
New York, NY 10003

Scott, Foresman and Co.
1900 East Lake Avenue
Glenview, IL 60025

Charles Scribner's Sons
597 Fifth Avenue
New York, NY 10017

Seabury Press
Episcopal Church Center
810 Second Avenue
New York, NY 10017

Seven Locks Press Inc.
Box 37
7425 MacArthur Boulevard
Cabin John, MD 20818

Sierra Club Books
2034 Fillmore Street
San Francisco, CA 94115

Starstream Books
630 Oakwood Avenue
Suite 119
West Hartford, CT 06110

Stemmer House
2627 Caves Road
Owings Mills, MD 21117

Frederick A. Stokes
10 East 53rd Street
New York, NY 10022

Teachers College Press
Columbia University
1234 Amsterdam Avenue
New York, NY 10027

Tundra Books of Northern
    New York
51 Clinton Street
P.O. Box 1030
Plattsburgh, NY 12901

Unicorn Books
(E.P. Dutton)
2 Park Avenue
New York, NY 10016

Viking Penguin, Inc.
40 West 23rd Street
New York, NY 10010

Walker & Co.
720 Fifth Avenue
New York, NY 10019

Wanderer Books
Simon & Schuster Building
1230 Avenue of the Americas
New York, NY 10020

Frederick Warne & Co., Inc.
2 Park Avenue
New York, NY 10016

Franklin Watts, Inc.
387 Park Avenue South
New York, NY 10016

Western Publishing Co.
1220 Mound Avenue
Racine, WI 53404

The Westminster Press
925 Chestnut Street
Philadelphia, PA 19107

Albert Whitman & Co.
5747 West Howard
Niles, IL 60648

Windmill Books
Simon & Schuster Building
1230 Avenue of the Americas
New York, NY 10020

Workman Publishing
    Company
1 West 39th Street
New York, NY 10018

Xerox Education Publications
245 Long Hill Road
Middletown, CT 06457

Index

A Big Fish Story, 36
A Is for Angry, 35
A Peaceable Kingdom: The Shaker Abecedarius, 63
A to Z Picture Book, 34, 35
A to Zoo Subject Guide to Children's Books, The, 167
Active listening, 22-23
Adventuring with Books, 167
All about Our 50 States, 104
Alphabears, 35
Alphabet the, and reading, 33-35
Alphabet books, 34-35
American Book Awards, 168
American Library Association, 104, 167, 195
An Edward Lear Alphabet, 35
Arbuthnot Anthology of Children's Literature, 65
Ashton-Warner, Sylvia, 85, 86
Auditory learner, 127, 128
Auditory problems, 135-137

B Is for Betsy, 61
Babbles, 17
Babies Need Books, 42
Barbe, Walter B., 130
Baum, L. Frank, 61, 106
Bears' ABC Book, The, 35
Beginning-to-read books, 35-36
  characteristics of, 35
Ben's Trumpet, 112
Bequest of Wings: A Family's Pleasure with Books, 42
Bernstein, Joanne E., 118
Bilingual instruction, 132
Blueberries for Sal, 162
Book awareness, 37
Book Finder: A Guide to Children's Literature, 167

Book recommendations
  biography and historical fiction, 189-192
  fantasy and science fiction, 183-185
  folktales and fairy tales, 173-175
  general fiction, 185-188
  general nonfiction, 192
  number and concept books, 170-172
  nursery rhymes, 169-170
  picture story books, 175-179
  poetry, 179-183
  series books, 188-189
  wordless picture books, 172-173
Books
  about food, 99-100
  about vehicles, 105
  appreciation of, 75-76
  finding, 159-160
  on historical topics, 107
Books in Print, 158
Bookclubs, 160-161
Bookmobiles, 149-150
Bookstores for children, 158-159
Book-sharing, 75
Boynton, Sandra, 35
Brian Wildsmith's ABC, 35
Brown Bear, Brown Bear, What Do You See?, 21
Bruno Munari's ABC, 35
Building blocks, 30-33
Butler, Dorothy, 42

Caldecott Medal, 167, 178
Caps for Sale, 82
Carle, Eric, 59, 60
Cat and Dog, 36
Cat at Bat, 36
Cauley, Lorinda Bryan, 97

Cause and effect, 73
Challenging books, 141-142
Chapter-a-day books, 61
Charlotte's Web, 61
Chickadee, 156
Childcraft, 65
Children who read early, 45
Children's Book Council, 165, 168, 196
Children's Book Showcase, 168
"Children's Choices," 165
Clark, Margaret, 45
Classical Calliope, 157
Clause, dependent, 21
Cobblestone, 156
Commercials, 123-124
Comparison of books, 75
Compound words, 89
Comprehension
  critical, 69
  inferential, 69
  levels of, 68-70
  literal, 68-69
  strategies of, 70-77
Concepts of print, 38
Consonants
  blends, 93
  initial, 92-93
Context
  learning words from, 82-83
Cookbooks for children, 97-98
Cooking and reading, 96-100
Cooperative Children's Book Center, 166
Cricket, 155
Curious George, 84

Dictation from children, 116-117
Digraphs, 93
Duff, Annis, 42
Durkin, Dolores, 45
Dysgraphia, 137-138
Dyslexia, 133

Early readers, 140-141
Eastman, P.D., 36, 94
Ebony Jr., 156
Estes, Eleanor, 61
Evaluation of books, 75

Everyday Enrichment, 143
Extending books, 162-163
Eye Winker, Tom Tinker, Chin Chopper, 23

Faces, 157
Fact and opinion, 73
Fiddle with a Riddle: Write Your Own Riddles, 118
Fingerplays, 23
Fisher, Aileen, 63
Flannel boards, 28-29, 59
Following written directions, 112-114
Food
  books about, 99-100
For Reading Out Loud!, 46, 49
  book recommendations from, 63-65
Freschet, Bernice, 36
Frog and Toad, 36
Fujikawa, Gyo, 34, 35, 60

Galdone, Paul, 75
Georgia Book Award, 169
Gifted Children Newsletter, 142-143
Gillilan, Strickland, 39
Ginger Pye, 61
Go, Dog, Go!, 36, 94
Goodman, Yetta, 26
Goodnight Owl, 36
Gordon, Ira, 17
Gordon, Thomas, 22
Group reading, 56-57

Hague, Kathleen, 35
Hall, Donald, 63
Hans Christian Andersen Award, 168
Haywood, Carolyn, 61
Henry, Marguerite, 61, 106
Heritage Songster, 23
Highlights for Children, 112, 155
Himler, Ronald, 36
Holophrase, 21
Holt, John, 24-25
Hop on Pop, 36
Horn Book, 166
How Children Learn, 24

204 *Growing Up Reading*

Humorous books, 120-121
Hutchins, Pat, 36

I Stood Upon a Mountain, 63
Isadora, Rachel, 112

Keats, Ezra Jack, 74,75
Keenan, Martha, 74
Key words, 85-86, 136
Kidwatching, 26-27
Kimmel, Margaret, 46
Kinesthetic learner, 128, 129, 130
Kobrin Letter, The, 166
Kunhardt, Dorothy, 58
Kuskin, Karla, 94, 112

Language
  as a social tool, 17
  envelope, 17
  scaffolding, 22
  structure of, 20-24
Lear, Edward, 35
Lenski, Lois, 141
Library programs
  infants and toddlers, 147
  preschoolers, 147-148
  school-age children, 148
Library
  reference resources, 150-152
  services, 152-153
  story hours, 147-148
Little Bear, 36
Little Red Hen, The, 75
Lobel, Arnold, 36

Magazines for children, 154-157
Magnetic alphabet letters, 34
Main idea, 71-72
Mannerly Adventures of Mistress Mouse, The, 74
McCloskey, Robert, 107, 162
Memory, 68
Minarik, Elsa H., 36
Mind's Eye, The, 56
Misty of Chincoteague, 61
Mock letters, 38, 117
Modality strengths, 127-130
Moose Baby, 36
Morris' Disappearing Bag, 74

Morrison, Bill, 118
Mr. Popper's Penguins, 61
Music
  reading and, 107-112
My Book House, 41, 65

National Geographic World, 156
Newbery Award, 167
Nutshell Library, 59

Odyssey, 156
One Fish, Two Fish, Red Fish, Blue Fish, 36, 94
Oral language development, 16-26, 37
Overgeneralization of rules, 24
Owl, 156
Owl at Home, 36
Ox-Cart Man, The, 63
Ozma of Oz, 61

Parent Effectiveness Training, 22
Parents' Choice, 166
Participation books, 58
Party ideas
  books about, 98
Pat the Bunny, 58
Patz, Nancy, 49
Pease Porridge Hot: A Mother Goose Cookbook, 97
Peet, Bill, 63, 120
Penny Power, 157
Pet Show, 74
Peter's Chair, 74
Philharmonic Gets Dressed, The, 112
Phonics, 91-94
Pickle in the Middle and Other Easy Snacks, 97
Picnics
  books about, 99
Picture books, 60-61
Ping-Pong technique, 17
Pinky Pye, 61
Play
  language development and, 30-33
Point-and-say books, 57-58
Predicting outcomes, 74

Growing Up Reading   205

Prefixes
　　common, 87-88
　　suffixes and, 86-87
Product labels and reading,
　　101-102
Provensen, Alice and Martin, 63
Pumpernickel Tickle and Mean Green Cheese, 49

Rachel and Obadiah, 74
Radlauer, Ruth, 105
Ranger Rick, 155
Rawlings, Marjorie Kinnard, 106
Read, Arnold Oren, 101
Read-aloud books
　　for infants, 57-58
　　for mature readers, 62
　　for multi-aged groups, 63-65
　　for preschoolers, 60-61
　　for primary grade children,
　　　61-62
　　for toddlers, 58-60
Read-Aloud Handbook, The, 46, 49
Reading aloud
　　emotional values of, 41
　　general guidelines, 47-50
　　impact of, 40-47
　　language development and,
　　　43-44
　　recommended books for,
　　　57-65
　　references on, 65-66
　　to infants, 50-51
　　to mature readers, 55-56
　　to preschoolers, 53-54
　　to primary grade children,
　　　54-55
　　to toddlers, 51-53
Reading difficulties, 130-140
　　psychological and educational
　　　factors in, 131-133
Reading Mother, The, 39
"Reading Rainbow," 119
Reading readiness, 15
　　checklist, 36-38
Reading routines, 146, 148
Reality and fantasy, 73-74
Resources for the Gifted, Inc., 142
Rey, H.A., 84

Rhyming games, 19-20
Riddle and joke books, 121
Roar and More, 94
Rockwell, Anne and Harlow, 103
Ronan, Margaret, 104
Rosie's Walk, 36

School libraries, 153-154
Segel, Elizabeth, 46
Sendak, Maurice, 59
Sequence and details, 72-73
Seuss, Dr., 36, 94
Shopping
　　lists, 100-101
　　reading and, 100-103
Sight words, 83-85
Skunk and Possum, 36
Slobodkina, Esphyr, 82
Slow readers, 138-140
Song
　　collection books, homemade,
　　　108-109
　　collections, 23
　　picture books, 110-112
Songbooks for children, 107-108
Songs and chants, 17-19
Squeeze a Sneeze, 118
Stadler, John, 36
Stone Soup, 157
Stormy, Misty's Foal, 61
Story schema, 72-73
Storytelling, 27-29
Subvocalizing, 134
Suffixes
　　common, 88-89
Supermarket, The, 103
Swassing, Raymond, 130
Syllables
　　rules for, 91

Tape recorder
　　tool for language growth, 29-30
Teacher, 85
Teaching Through Modality Strengths: Concepts and Practices, 130
Telegraphic speech, 21
Television
　　adventure and drama, 121
　　children and, 45-46, 118-124

   mystery and fantasy, 122-123
   science and nature, 121-122
   sports, 122
   vocabulary and, 26
Tether, Graham, 36
Thinking Cap, 143
365 New Words for Kids Calendar, 86
Traveling and reading, 103-107
Trelease, Jim, 46
Turkle, Brinton, 74, 107

Van Steenwyck, Elizabeth, 104
Very Hungry Caterpillar, The, 59
Visual learner, 127, 128, 129
Visual problems, 133-135
Vocabulary enhancers, 25
Vowel sounds, 93-94

Wake Up, Jeremiah, 36
Webbing, 162
Wee Sing, 23

Wells, Rosemary, 74
Weston Woods, 54, 72
What's in a Name: Famous Brand Names, 101
White, E.B., 61
Wild, Robin, 35
Wilder, Laura Ingalls, 106
Wildsmith, Brian, 35, 60
Wilie, Joanne, 36
Wizard of Oz, The, 61
Word games, 26, 90-91
Writing
   for children, 115-117
   independent, 117-118
   reading and, 114-118

Yearling, The, 106
Young Fluent Readers, 45
Your Big Backyard, 155

Zeifel, Frances, 97

Growing Up Reading

About the Author

Linda Leonard Lamme is Professor of Elementary and Early Childhood Education at the University of Florida. She received her Ph.D. from Syracuse University. Dr. Lamme is the senior author of *Raising Readers* (Walker & Co., 1980), *Learning to Love Literature* (National Council of Teachers of English, 1981), and *Growing Up Writing* (Acropolis Books, Ltd., 1984). She is an active member of the International Reading Association, the National Association for the Education of Young Children, and the National Council of Teachers of English. Dr. Lamme, her daughter and son, and her husband enjoy reading as a family.